FANTASTIC FEATS AND *Ridiculous* RECORDS

BARRON'S

First edition for North America published in 2009
by Barron's Educational Series, Inc.

Copyright © 2009 Arcturus Publishing Limited

First published in 2009 by Arcturus Publishing Limited
26/27 Bickels Yard, 151–153 Bermondsey Street
London SE1 3HA

Author: Adam Phillips
Editor: Fiona Tulloch
Designer: Mike Reynolds

All inquiries should be addressed to:
Barron's Educational Series, Inc.
250 Wireless Boulevard
Hauppauge, New York 11788
www.barronseduc.com

ISBN-13: 978-0-7641-4338-0
ISBN-10: 0-7641-4338-7

CH000698EN

Library of Congress Catalog Card No.: 2009925372

Printed in the United States of America
9 8 7 6 5 4 3 2

FANTASTIC FEATS AND *Ridiculous* RECORDS

Adam Phillips

BARRON'S

Quotation sources:

10 Boomer Hodel to *Daily Mail*, Oct 2008; **11** (t) Alexei Sharshkov to Reuters, Apr 2006; **11** (b) Nicolas Campos Sanchez to *Short News*, June 2007; **12** Karen Quigley to *USA Today*, June 2008; **13** Lou Ann Best to Rex Features, Jan 2009; **14** Crystal Socha to the American Paint Horse Association, Dec 2008; **18** Nancy Solchenberger to KUSA*TV, May 2007; **20** Alexander Nedo to BBC, April 2002; **23** Kenji Kawakamai to *J@pan Inc.*, Apr 2002; **24** The World Toilet Association: www.worldtoilet.org; **25** Mike Ross to *Wired Magazine*, 2007; **29** (t) Mark Cernicky writing for *Cycle World*, June 2007; **29** (b) Duncan Everson to *Manawatu Standard*, June 2008; **31** Serginho Laus to *National Geographic*, Feb 2005; **32** Alain Robert: www.alainrobert.com; **34** David Kirke to *Daily Telegraph*, July 2004; **36** (t) Yves Rossy to *The Times*, Sept 2008; **36** (b) Markus Stoeckl to Red Bull, Sept 2008; **38** Travis Pastrana to www.motorcross.com, Apr 2008; **39** (t) Aaron Fotheringham to *The Sun*, Nov 2008; **39** (b) Hartley Hughes to BBC, Dec 1998; **40** Ken Block to *Rally Sport*, Apr 2008; **42** (t) Ray Moon to Reuters, Sept 2008; **42** (b) Dr. Bernard Morzol to CNN, Sept 2008; **43** Joey Chestnut to *Tampa Tribune*, Jul 2008; **44** Elaine Davidson to *Closer*, Jul 2007; **44** Manuel Uribe to *Daily Record*, Oct 2008; **46** Ateng Koswara to *Daily Telegraph* Aug, 2008; **46** Cathie Jung to *The Sun*, Aug 2007; **48** Georges Christen to *The West Australian*, June 2007; **49** (t) Larry Ramos Gomez to David Staples, Feb 2008; **49** (b) Aniket Chindak to *Daily Record*, Jan 2008; **51** (t) Wim Hof to *China Daily*, Dec 2008; **51** (b) Darren Taylor: www.professorsplash.com; **52** (t) Gary Turner to *Independent On Sunday*, Oct 2005; **52** (b) Dennis Avner to *The Sun*, Sept 2008; **54** Prince Philip to Tommy Mattinson, June 2008; **57** (t) Mainichi Daily News: http://mdn.mainichi.jp; **57** (b) Li Yang in *Crazy English* (documentary) 1999; **58** (t) Chris Hodgkins, writing for BBC, May 2008; **58** (b) Won Park to Dean Murray, Jan 2009; **60** La Tomatina Festival: www.tomatina.net; **61** Pam Barker to Associated Press, Jan 2006; **62** Wife Carrying World Championship: www.sonkajarvi.fi; **63** Zac Monro to *The Times*, Sept 2006; **65** Georgina Turner writes for *The Guardian*, Nov 2005; **69** Joe Hedrick to *Star Tribune*, Jul 2008; **71** Mark Cleland to *Irish Examiner*, Aug 2008; **72** Mac Davis: wwwsummerredneckgames.com; **73** Phil Shaw in his book *Extreme Ironing* (2003); **75** Gustav Temple to *Daily Telegraph*, Jul, 2007; **77** Roy Waung to www.starwars.com, Jan 2007; **79** Ralph Hannah to ITN News, Oct 2008; **81** Edna Arvidson to Associated Press, Feb 2007; **82** Justin Shorb to *Powell Tribune*, Sept 2008; **83** Duncan Best to BBC, Oct 2008; **84** (t) Joe Jaina to www.savethechildren.org.uk, July 2008; **84** (b) anonymous competitor to *The Daily Telegraph* (Australia), Sept 2008; **86** Mark McGown writing for Clublet, Sept 2005; **87** Dorothy Wilson to *Daily Telegraph*, Sept 2008; **88** Andreas Kirsch to Reuters Television, Jan 2009; **89** Le Trung to *The Star*, Dec 2008; **91** SH, writing for *The Times*, Sept 2007; **92** Coney Island Sideshow School: www.coneyisland.com/sideshow_school; **93** (t) Ilker Yilmaz to Associated Press, Sept 2004; **93** (b) Kanchana Ketkaew to *The Telegraph*, Jan 2009; **94** Ashrita Furman in the book *Tricks of the Trade for Kids* (1994); **95** (t) Norman Gary, BBC website, March 2009; **95** (b) Tiana Walton to the *Daily Mail*, Aug 2008.

Picture credits:

5 REUTERS/Rick Wilking; **9** (t) David Jones/PA Archive/PA Photos, (b) REUTERS/Sukree Sukplang; **10** Clark Little/SWNS.com; **11** (t) AP Photo/Ivan Sekretarev, (b) AP Photo/Martin Mejia; **12** (t) Deanne Fitzmaurice/San Francisco Chronicle/Corbis, (b) Peter Byrne/PA; **13** Timothy A. Clary/AFP/Getty Images; **14** (t) Frösö Zoo Sweden/www.frosozoo.se, (b) AP Photo/The Wichita Eagle, Mike Hutmacher; **15** AP Photo/Xinhua, Zhang Jianhua; **16** (t) AP Photo/Jacquelyn Martin, (b) AP Photo/Matthew S. Gunby; **17** (t) Barcroft Media/Sam Barcroft, (b) Sarah Rice/Star Ledger/Corbis; **18** (t) Andrew Aiken/Rex Features, (b) REUTERS/Rick Wilking; **20** (t) CTK Czech News Agency/CTK/PA Photos, (b) ABACA ABACA Press/ABACA/PA Photos; **21** (t) AP Photo/Rick Rycroft, (b) AP Photo/Luisa Ferreira; **22** (t) Everett Kennedy Brown/epa/Corbis, (b) Jackie Fox/fotoLibra; **23** (t) AP Photo/Katsumi Kasahara, (b) Mark Obstfeld/UPPA/Photoshot; **24** (t) REUTERS/Jo Yong hak, (b) Mark Obstfeld/UPPA/Photoshot; **25** (r) Trixie Textor/Getty Images, (l) REUTERS/Leonhard Foeger; **26** (t) Patrick Pleul/epa/Corbis, (b) Patrick Pleul/UPPA/Photoshot; **27** (t) REUTERS/Krishnendu Halder, (b) REUTERS/Eliseo Fernandez; **28** AP Photo/Frank Hormann; **29** (t) Transtock/Corbis, (b) Barcroft Media/Chris Gorman; **31** (t) Barcroft Media/Incredible Features, (b) Gregg Newton/Corbis; **32** REUTERS/Rickey Rogers; **33** (t) Joao Abreu Miranda/epa/Corbis, (b) REUTERS/Joerg Mitter/Pool; **34** (t) Ken McKay/Rex Features, (b) Tony Kyriacou/Rex Features; **35** (t) Reuters/CORBIS, (b) ALBERT GEA/Reuters/Corbis; **36** (t) REUTERS/Denis Balibouse, (b) Alfredo Escobar/epa/Corbis; **37** (t) AP Photo/Hermann J. Knippertz, (b) AP Photo/Plain Dealer, Brynne Shaw; **38** (t) REUTERS/Phil McCarten, (b) REUTERS/Francisco Bonilla; **39** (t) Barcroft Media/Barry Bland, (b) PA Archive/PA Photos; **40** Tim Zimmerman Photography; **42** (t) REUTERS/Mick Tsikas, (b) Ben Curtis/PA Archive/PA Photos; **43** (tr) Lindsey Parnaby/Empics Entertainment/PA Photos, (tl) William Thomas Cain/Getty Images, (br) Henny Ray Abrams/AP/PA Photos; **44** (t) REUTERS/David Moir, (b) REUTERS/Tomas Bravo; **45** (l) China Photos/Getty Images, (r) ChinaFotoPress/Li Shuangqi/UPPA/Photoshot; **46** (t) REUTERS/Supri, (b) AP Photo/Frank Franklin II; **47** REUTERS/Luke MacGregor; **48** (t) Action Press/Rex Features, (b) LEE Besford/Reuters/Corbis; **49** (t) Charles Sykes/Rex Features, (b) Barcroft Media/Simon De Trey-White; **50** (t) Everett Kennedy Brown/epa/Corbis, (b) ITV/Rex Features; **51** (t) Barcroft Media/Henny Boogert, (b) Barcroft Media/Michael Martin; **52** (t) Geoffrey Swaine/Rex Features, (b) Brad Barket/Getty Images; **54** (t) Anthony Devlin/PA Wire, (b) Arthur Edwards/The Sun/PA; **55** (t) AP Photo/Denis Poroy, (b) Barcroft Media/Zoom Multimedia; **56** REUTERS/Kim Kyung-Hoon; **57** (t) REUTERS/Toru Hanai, (b) China Photos/Reuters/Corbis; **58** (t) REUTERS/Darren Staples, (b) Rex Features; **59** (t) Philippe Eranian/CORBIS, (b) REUTERS/Crack Palinggi; **60** (tl) Biel Aliño/EFE/UPPA/Photoshot, (tr) AP Photo/Santiago Lyon; **61** (tl) REUTERS/Albert Gea, (br) AP Photo/The Sun Journal, Russ Dillingham; **62** (t) Rungroj Yongrit/epa/Corbis, (b) Tommi Korpihalla/AFP/Getty Images; **63** (tl) REUTERS/David Moir, (c) REUTERS/Jeff J Mitchell, (b) Mauri Ratilainen/epa/Corbis; **65** (t) REUTERS/Tobias Schwarz, (b) David Cannon/Getty Images for Etihad Airways; **66** (t) ChinaFotoPress/Photocome/PA Photos, (b) REUTERS/Jo Yong-Hak; **67** (t) Barry Batchelor/PA Archive/PA Photos, (b) Katja Lenz/DPA/PA Photos; **68** (t) imago sportfotodienst/Talking Sport/Photoshot, (b) AP Photo/Sakchai Lalit; **69** (t) Philippe Hays/Rex Features, (b) REUTERS/Nir Elias; **70** (t) Laurence Griffiths/Getty Images, (b) AP Photo/Keystone, Jean-Christophe Bott; **71** (t) REUTERS/Mark Blinch, (b) Kirsty Wigglesworth/AFP/Getty Images; **72** Sol Neelman/Corbis; **73** (t) Johnny Green/PA Archive/PA Photos, (b) Michael St. Maur Sheil/Corbis; **74** (t) AP Photo/Max Nash, (b) Peter Schneider/AP/PA Photos; **75** (cl) Jeff Moore/Empics Entertainment/Jeff Moore, (tr) Rex Features; **77** (t) REUTERS/Gus Ruelas, (b) Matteo Rossetti/Rex Features; **78** (t) REUTERS/Str Old, (b) REUTERS/Toshi Maeda; **79** REUTERS/Jorge Adorno; **80** (t) Wim Beddegenoodts/Reporters/UPPA/Photoshot, (b) REUTERS/Stringer Shanghai; **81** (t) AP Photo/Will Kincaid, (b) REUTERS/David Gray; **82** (t) Barcroft Media/Norman Kent, (b) Barcroft Media; **83** (t) Jonathan Hordle/Rex Features, (b) Andy Rain/epa/Corbis; **84** (t) AP Photo/Lefteris Pitarakis, (b) Tess Peni/Rex Features; **86** (t) Ray Tang/Rex Features, (b) Zhang Xiuke/ChinaPhotoPress/Photocome/PA Photos; **87** REUTERS/Phil Noble; **88** (t) REUTERS/Alex Grimm, (b) REUTERS/Nicky Loh; **89** (t) Barcroft Media, (b) Frank Leonhardt/dpa/Corbis; **90** (t) Everett Kennedy Brown/epa/Corbis, (b) Reuters/CORBIS; **91** (t) Reuters/Corbis, (b) Barcroft Media/Mark Wessels; **92** (t) REUTERS/Mike Segar, (b) Leon Schadeberg/Rex Features; **93** (t) AP Photo/Osman Orsal, (b) REUTERS/Sukree Sukplang; **94** REUTERS/Zainal Abd Halim; **95** (t) Sipa Press/Rex Features, (b) Andrew Price/Rex Features.

Mouse Houses!

It may not be a luxury penthouse suite at the top of a gleaming skyscraper, but the humble tennis ball is helping keep the British harvest mouse alive. The mouse is so tiny that the cute critter (known formally as *micromys minutus*) is incredibly difficult for wildlife experts to keep a count of. Because of its size and the fact that it only weighs about the same as a small coin, it's not only Britain's smallest mouse but also Britain's tastiest snack for hungry predators (well, probably). This risk of being gobbled up led to the mice building nests above ground in tall grass to protect themselves. With intensive farming methods believed to be threatening the species' habitat too, the U.K.-based Wildlife Trust needed to come up with an ingenious way to help keep the mice safe and ended up taking their inspiration from Mother Nature. Copying the mice's cunning plan, the Wildlife Trust decided the best way to protect, accommodate, and count them was to use tennis balls. They make a single hole in the ball and suspend it above the ground before inserting a seed into it. Inevitably, the mouse finds its way in and can live safely while the wildlife experts monitor their numbers. Just like they do with Tim, pictured here, who lives on high in Bristol, in southwest England.

The balls used to shelter the mice come from Wimbledon, the home of one of the world's greatest tennis tournaments.

Move Over, Kermit!

Performing frogs are something of a rarity—unless they're made from cloth and are being pursued by Miss Piggy. So when Nong Oui, a black-spotted female frog, was shown to reporters in Pattaya, Thailand, she caused quite a splash. Able to sit on a toy motorbike and more than happy to be handled, the frog became a nationwide hit. But it's one of Nong's other talents that has caused even more of a stir—her owner claims that the amazing frog can predict the National Lottery numbers. By looking for numbers in the patterns on Nong's skin, locals have discovered the winning numbers for ten lotteries in a row. Expect crowds to start forming around Nong Oui's home... just don't try to cut in line!

Nong the frog used to be fed pork and chicken by her owner, before being moved onto proper frog food.

STAR ENTRY

Most Absurd Animal

"Running on a wheel isn't enough for Fin and Tofu – they like a more extreme rush,"
explains owner and rat surfing trainer Boomer Hodel.

They're best known for causing the spread of the bubonic plague and being feared by housewives (and husbands) the world over. But some lucky rats end up living the lifestyle that most people would die for!

Sunny weather, warm water, the perfect beach, and surfing—sounds like the ideal vacation, but it's actually the lifestyle that two rats, Fin and Tofu, enjoy on a regular basis in Hawaii, thanks to their 14-year-old owner, Boomer Hodel. The lucky rats go surfing twice a week for 20 minutes at a time

and bedazzle stunned onlookers as they ride 4-foot/1.2-m waves and perform tricks such as surfing through "tubes" (tunnels of water).

Boomer discovered his rats loved water when he took them down to the beach to wash them. Then after breaking his surfboard, he decided to create two new boards from the wreckage for the long-tailed toothy twosome. Thanks to Boomer's training, the one-year-old rats now fall off their boards less than most human surfers.

The two rats are kept on a high-protein, low-carbohydrate diet to help keep them in tip-top shape for the rigors of surfing.

LIKE A DUCK TO WATER Fin and Tofu are at no risk from the water because rats love to swim—as proven by a runaway rat off the coast of New Zealand in 2005 who had been radio tagged by scientists for a study. He tried to make a break for freedom and swam 1,312 feet/400 m before the scientists managed to recapture him! Some reckon the intrepid swimmer could have set a new world record for the distance covered by a rat swimming in open water.

Piggy in the Middle

Twelve little piggies went to Moscow...to participate in the third annual Pig Olympics in 2006. Attracting entrants from seven different countries, including South Africa and Ukraine, the special Olympics were made up of three events: a running race featuring obstacles and jumps; pigball, where a ball is pasted with fish oil to encourage the swine to push it around until it lands in a goal; and a new swimming event, that saw the pigs paddling from one side of a pool to the other. Unfortunately, the piglets were better at bumping into each other than actually swimming in a straight line.

Pig-boxing may be introduced at the 2009 Pig Olympics.

Those worried that the pigs are being treated cruelly can rest easy, as zoo psychologists were on hand to monitor the porky athletes.

"They don't get eaten. How could you eat a competitor who is known around the world?"
—*Alexei Sharshkov, vice president of the Sport-Pig Federation, when asked if the piglets are eaten after participating in the Olympics.*

Fashion Victims

It is believed that the English name for the rodent, "guinea," came from the amount of money you had to pay for the furry critter when it was introduced into Britain in the old days. A guinea was a British coin used in the late 1600s.

Whereas the Western world likes its guinea pigs playing in their cages and being adorable pets, the people of Peru prefer theirs (known there as *cuy*) dressed up in traditional Peruvian dresses for the annual Festival of the Guinea Pig in Huacho, Peru. The furry creatures are dressed up as miners, peasants, queens, and kings and are then judged on who is the best-dressed. Pictured here in traditional folk singer attire is the 2008 festival winner, Yasmina del Amor. Which is the name of the guinea pig, and not its owner, of course.

"This isn't common. We're very proud of it."
Festival-goer Nicolas Campos Sanchez on the tradition of dressing up guinea pigs.

Who You Calling Ugly?

If dogs could read, the World's Ugliest Dog contest could have serious effects on their self-esteem. Thankfully they can't read, so we can have a good-natured (and guilt-free) laugh at their expense each year at the World's Ugliest Dog Festival at the Sonoma-Marin Fair in Petaluma, California. Dog owners from across the USA travel to the contest to show off their pets' "challenging" looks. Pictured here is the 2007 winner, Elwood, a two-year-old Chinese Crested–Chihuahua, who traveled from New Jersey all the way to California to take part in the competition. And yes, his tongue always hangs out like that because he has no teeth on the left-hand side of his mouth.

The 2008 winner, Gus from Florida, had just one eye after a fight with a tomcat, no hair at all, and only three legs after his ongoing fight with skin cancer. His owners used the prize money of $1,600 to pay for his radiation therapy.

"I think he's proud of who he is. There's a prance in his step that is very confident," *explains Karen Quigley, owner of Elwood, the World's Ugliest Dog 2007.*

Hamster Escapes A Hammering

Cats are supposed to have nine lives, but judging from Mike the hamster's escapades in 2006, furry rodents must run a close second. After all, he managed to survive going through a shredder and three different kinds of crushing machinery during his death-defying journey at the industrial waste unit on Deeside in North Wales. He was spun, shaken, and nearly crushed to death before popping out the other end of the four-minute process, which is normally used to destroy washing machines (and not accommodate small mammals).

No one is sure how he ended up at the plant, but workers were amazed to find that Mike had only a sore foot to show for his ordeal. He is now the pet of proud owner, schoolboy Liam Bull (pictured right).

In 2006, Cheshire firefighters had to use high-tech cutting tools to rescue a hamster whose head had become wedged between the bars of its cage.

WHEELIE LUCKY You'd normally expect to see broken-down cars on the hard shoulder of Britain's highways, but in 2006, motorists were amazed to see a hamster running along one inside a plastic exercise ball on the notoriously dangerous M6. He was later rescued by animal welfare workers who believed he must have dropped out of a car by accident. He was subsequently named Roly—and, luckily, was not prosecuted for driving without a license.

The original squirrel was called Twiggy because she ate all the leaves off the Bests' houseplants, leaving behind just twigs!

Water Amazing Squirrel!

To old people, Twiggy is the name of a mini-skirt-wearing supermodel from 1960s London; to animal lovers, Twiggy is a squirrel from Florida who has been trained to water-ski by the Best family since the late '70s. Actually, Twiggy isn't a single squirrel who has been waterskiing for the last 30 years—the average life span of a squirrel is just five to six years after all—but a series of squirrels who go by the same name.

The very first squirrel was found as a baby by Chuck and Lou Ann Best after a hurricane had blown it out of its nest. Then, after buying a remote-controlled boat and blaming his new toy on wanting to teach Twiggy to water-ski, Chuck actually thought it might be a good idea. Fast-forward to the present day and Twiggy the squirrel has appeared on many TV shows and in commercials, and even starred in hit Hollywood movies such as *Dodgeball* and *Anchorman*.

Chuck and Lou Ann Best have also trained other animals to water-ski, including an armadillo, two French poodles, and two miniature horses. They also taught a chimpanzee to roller skate!

"Twiggy is really quite happy with her life. She has her own room at home with trees to climb, and has the run of my motor home while we're on the road."
Lou Ann Best, dismissing complaints from animal rights campaigners.

Pygmy Me Up and Cuddle Me!

Although the baby albino pygmy marmoset monkey pictured here is officially the world's smallest living monkey, it could easily take the award for being the most cute as well—if such things could be measured by scientists. As for actual physical measurements, well, this South American specimen will weigh 3.5 ounces/100 g and measure a mere 13.7 inches/ 35 cm when fully grown.

Although the marmoset looks adorable, its name is believed to be an old French word that means "grotesque image."

You're looking at the picture and we know exactly what you're thinking: "I want one!" Well, be warned—although the idea of owning a cute monkey is appealing, the reality is somewhat different. Expect a monkey to bite, scratch, cause damage, poop all over the house, and cost a fortune. Expert owners recommend you buy two monkeys so they keep each other company to stave off depression. Double the fun!

The monkey featured here was born at the Froso Zoo in Switzerland in 2006—he was one of a pair but sadly, the only one to survive.

The Braid-y Bunch

THE MANE'S A PAIN It's believed that Summer's mane could be a world record breaker too. In the past, it has been known to get tangled up in Summer's mouth while she was eating. It explains why her mane ends look chewed off in places!

It's very wise that the owner of Summer the American paint horse keeps her beloved animal's tail braided and covered in a tube sock when she's not showing her off. After all, the tail in question measures a record-breaking 12.5 feet/3.81 m and could cause one or two slip-ups when cantering across fields.

Summer's extraordinary tail is combed and shampooed every two months; owner Crystal Socha has to put aside three hours to accomplish this Herculean task because each hair is as fine as a fishing line!

"I don't think I've ever gotten every knot out of that tail. It takes a lot longer in the summer when she's flicking at flies. When it's out and it's flowing, then I know why it's worth it," said Summer's owner, Crystal Socha.

Cat-astrophically Fat

These days you could be forgiven for thinking that the world's fattest cats live on Wall Street, but you would be wrong—fat cats of the feline kind are (just about) alive and (barely) kicking all over the world. Although there are no longer any official records—experts believe such a record would encourage people to overfeed their animals—there are many candidates out there desperately vying for the world's attention.

Pictured here is Xu Jirong from China and his cat who weighs in at 33 pounds/15 kg and has a waist size of 30 inches/ 77 cm. But that cat is dwarfed by Katy, a Siamese cat living in the Ural mountains in Russia, who weighs about 50 pounds/ 22.5 kg. Her owner claims that she doesn't eat much but says she can wolf down a hot dog in less than a minute...

Snowball the nuclear cat shot to fame in 2001 when her owner Rodger Degagne claimed he had found her wandering around a deserted nuclear facility—and it was because of radiation that Snowball had ended up weighing a huge 87 pounds/39.4 kg. The story later turned out to be a hoax!

FELINE FAN MAIL

Perhaps the most infamous fat cat in the world was Tiddles, a stray cat who was adopted by June Watson, a toilet attendant at Paddington Station in London, England. Tiddles ended up weighing the same as a six-year-old boy, and became a star who received letters and the finest in haute cuisine from his many fans. While he went on to be declared London Fat Cat Champion in 1982, he was put to sleep the following year because of his obesity.

Get a Pet-icure

If you want the perfect set of feet, then you'll need 5,000 flesh-eating fish at a cost of $50,000 to do the job. Or, at least, that's what salon owner Yvonne Le decided when razors were banned for use in pedicures in the state of Virginia, where Yvonne's Hair & Nails salon is based. She and her husband, John Ho, scoured the Internet to find an alternative to using a blade and hit the jackpot—they came across the garra rufa fish that are known as Doctor Fish because they are used in the treatment of ailments such as eczema.

So far, the fish have nibbled the dead skin off 6,000 pairs of feet.

   With the fish bought from China, customers have flocked to the salon to experience the toothless nips of the tiny carp that set about removing the dead skin from feet over a 15-30-minute period. According to customers, the sensation of the fish nibbling away at the scaly skin on their feet has been described as small, delicate kisses. Fishy kisses, obviously.

   And as for that initial $50,000 investment made by the couple? Well, John believes they could make $500,000 a year from their finned friends...

Canine on Canvas

The very idea might have had Van Gogh cutting off his other ear in despair, but the artistic creations of three dogs trained to help the disabled at Shore Service Dogs in Britain are winning fans nonetheless. Trained by their owner Mary Stadelbacher, the dogs are able to paint bright and "abstract" paintings by holding the brush in their mouths. The resulting work has fetched up to approximately $345.00/£230 per picture from the paying public.

Each dog-painted picture is signed with a black paw print by the canine artist responsible for the masterpiece.

"Go paint, Sammy!" *calls Mary Stadelbacher to her dog during painting demonstrations.*

Stadelbacher doesn't claim that her dogs are the first to put paw to paint—there have been many examples of animals exhibiting their artistic skills—but she does believe that her three dogs may well be the first canines to use an actual brush.

Ninja Chimp

If he were still alive, even the master of showbiz martial arts, Bruce Lee, might be eyeing Charlie the chimpanzee rather nervously. And so he should, because the 17-year-old chimp is the proud recipient of a karate black belt. His owner, Carmen Presti, noticed the chimp's interest in martial arts when she was working out at a local karate studio. Soon, Charlie began picking up all the moves, including kicking and punching.

In 1987, the martial arts monkey was awarded a black belt for his amazing display of skill. He now enjoys the high life—in between touring the U.S. and showing off his famous jump spinning heel kick, he has appeared on *Larry King Live* and the Ricki Lake show as well as in numerous advertisements.

Charlie weighs an astonishing 198 pounds/90 kg. Bruce Lee was believed to weigh around 132 pounds/60 kg.

In between martial arts bouts, Charlie likes to relax by playing in his pool, reading magazines, and eating blue cheese pizza and chicken wings.

STIFF COMPETITION Charlie looks like he may have an archrival in the shape of a 12-year-old monkey in Japan who can karate chop panels of wood in two and spar with his sensei (martial arts teacher) in between serving drinks at his sensei's bar in Japan. Father of two Yachan is trained by his monkey-breeding owner on a daily basis, doing sit-ups, push-ups, and rope-jumping.

My Very Little, Teeny Tiny Pony

Fans of horse riding may not be enamored with Thumbelina, the world's smallest living horse, because she is only 17 inches/44 cm across. But for everyone else, this seven-year-old dwarf miniature horse would be the perfect pet to take for a walk in the park to the bemusement of passersby. The miniature ("mini") horse breed is small enough to begin with, but because Thumbelina is a dwarf too, she is extra special and is nicknamed Mini Mini by her owners.

Owner Michael Goessling says that Thumbelina likes the company of his dogs as well as the other 50 horses in his stable and is well known for bossing the horses around in between playing with the dogs.

THE END OF MINI MINI? It was feared that Thumbelina may have perished in the floods that hit her home, Goose Creek Farms in Missouri, when the creek broke its levies in September 2008. Thankfully, the quick-footed mother of owner Michael raced to the barn where Thumbelina is kept and lifted her out of the water, saving her. Not bad for a 67-year-old lady!

Your Dinner's in the Goat!

Think of goats and you might think of cheese, milk, their tendency to eat anything, or perhaps even their fiery temperament. But what you might not know about goats is that they help local Moroccan woman make Argan oil. It's true!

These amazing goats feed on the delicious berries found high in Argan trees, but to get to them they have to scale some seriously tall trees. So what's the gross part? Well, once the goats have eaten their fill, they poo out the kernels of the berry seed. These kernels are picked up by the local women and then ground to make Argan oil. You can then buy the oil and use it in the kitchen, or, grosser still, you can rub it onto the skin as a beauty treatment!

Not all Argan oil is produced using goat droppings—modern machinery can make the oil directly from the berries. It's just not quite the same...

Pooch Smooch

The record set in Littleton smashed the previous record held by the Netherlands, where only a paltry 27 pooches were wed.

Some people call it puppy love—but possibly not the 356 dogs who turned up to be married in Littleton, Colorado, in 2007, when they became the participants in several arranged marriages organized by their owners. The big day saw the dogs swapping their usual collars for full wedding gear, including tuxedos and wedding dresses (stop cringing!), and then taking what was known as their "bow-wow vows."

If you're feeling inspired by the Littleton mass mutt marriage, then you can do it for your pets too. If you want reassurance that your mutt has found the right mate, then why not consult a pet marriage counselor? Then, once your pooch pal is lined up with the perfect partner, why not hire a dog wedding planner to arrange the big day? For $1,000, you'll get smart outfits, a marriage license, and even a cake. We are not making this up.

"It was time to make it legal. Dezi is totally in love with Lucy. They are both almost two years old and they've been living together the whole time." Nancy Solchenberger, proud mother-of-the-dog-bride.

YOU CANNOT BE SERIOUS... A top tip from dog wedding experts: Although the dog's wedding dress may look splendid when held up for all to see, the design may not work in the horizontal position when your loved-up lassie is walking. So now you know what to look for...

Objects of Ridicule

Useless, oversized, undersized, bizarrely shaped—if you can think of an everyday object, then you can guarantee it's been "ridiculized"...

Want to ride on the most original bicycle? Find the perfect solution for a runny nose? Or better still, read the world's smallest book at bedtime using an electron microscope?

Well, it would seem you're not alone. For years, madcap inventors from around the world have been busy in their workshops, dreaming up all kinds of alternatives to everyday items. Some have even forgone regular 9-to-5 careers (and most of their spare time, too) to dedicate their lives to making the world laugh.

In this chapter, we look at the objects that we all usually take for granted but, because of such "trailblazing" individuals, can now be seen in an entirely new light. Whether it be a guitar-shaped bike (see page 26), a mega-sized game of Monopoly (see page 21), or the world's longest toilet paper roll (see page 24), there really is something out there for everybody...

Eye Strain Guaranteed!

Just the size of a match head, the world's smallest commercially produced book was introduced on the market back in 2002. Published by German company Die-Gestalten Verlag, the 0.09 x 0.11 inch/2.4 x 2.9 mm book was created by the typographer Josua Reichert and boasts 26 pages. To avoid losing it in the mail (or in one's pocket), the leather-bound book is delivered in a mahogany box, and a magnifying glass is also included so you can actually read the contents. Tweezers to turn the tiny pages are, sadly, not included. As to what the book's contents actually are, well, check out the black box below. If you did decide to buy a copy, you should know that they are currently selling for around $100.

"It was printed in the usual way, but all the machinery and tools had to be created in miniature first." Publisher of the world's smallest commercially produced book, Alexander Nedo.

Nano Book

There could be a new challenger to the world's smallest book, that has arrived in the absurdly small shape of *Teeny Ted From Turnip Town*, a children's book written by Malcolm Douglas Chaplin. To read it, you will need to buy an electron microscope because it is so small—in fact, you can't see the book with the human eye. It's 0.003 x 0.004 inches/ 0.07 x 0.1 mm, and is made up of 30 carved tablets placed side by side. There's only one in existence at this time, but its creators, Karen Kavanagh and Li Yang, are hoping to publish more—with each one costing around $20,000.

STOP READING NOW...

... if you don't want to know the plot of this bonsai book. For the rest of us, well, it's not a murder mystery or a fantasy book in the style of J. K. Rowling. Nope, on each page of the book is a letter of the alphabet. And we all know how that ends!

More Memory, Less Size

Electronics manufacturers are happy to feed our obsession for buying the latest gadgets in their smallest form, but trying to make something as complicated as a tiny but reliable hard drive is a tough proposition. Step forward Toshiba, who released the world's smallest hard drive back in 2004. The ridiculously small but cool 0.85-inch/ 2.15-cm hard drive weighed a mere 0.004 pound/2 g and featured a storage capacity of 4GB. Not satisfied with that, though, Toshiba unveiled a version in 2007 (pictured here) that boasted 8GB!

The hard drive has already been used in a cell phone released by Toshiba in Japan. The company reckoned that 2,000 songs could be stored on the 4GB hard drive.

If you want to play the oversized board game yourself, then head to Monopoly In The Park in San Jose, California. The 926-square-foot/86-sq-m board is officially the largest outdoor version of Monopoly in the world. Expect to wear huge token-shaped hats and to wear a prison outfit if you're sent to jail.

Mega Monopoly

There's nothing quite so boring as a board game played with your family. Monopoly can be the exception to this rule, though, as it can lead to all-out family feuds about property prices and huge debt. And when it comes to huge, the massive Monopoly board that was displayed at the Sydney Home Show in Australia in 2005 is as large as it gets. Measuring a massive 4,736 square feet/440 sq m, the board earned a world record for being the biggest of its type. The hotels and houses, which make up a key part of the game, are a whopping 1,700 times larger than the ones used in the regular board game. The only thing that could be a problem is the need for a professional home-moving service when you need to place them on the massive board!

More than 5,120,000,000 of the green houses that are featured in Monopoly have been made since the board game was first introduced in 1935.

MAD FOR MONOPOLY Think that Monopoly can drag sometimes? Then imagine setting the record for the longest game of Monopoly in history—a whopping 70 hours. As for other board games, if you prefer to play them in the bath, then to beat the record, you'd have to play for more than 99 hours while fending off bars of soap and rubber ducks; and if you're partial to playing in a tree house, you'd need to beat 286 hours. Finally, for any vampires reading who like to play while upside down, you'll have to beat 26 hours!

Table for 16,000, Please

There was no fear of boring conversation if you were one of the people who took part in setting the new record for the world's longest dining table ever laid, back in 1998. After all, the 3-mile/5-km table seated 16,000 diners and spanned a third of the then new Vasco da Gama bridge in Lisbon, Portugal. Guests enjoyed a traditional Portuguese dish, the famous Feijoada stew...all 10 tons of it, in fact. If they looked closely, diners might have spotted the odd pig snout or two floating in it, too. It is hoped that those who decided that snouts were not their favorite dinner were too polite to complain to the host...

The event was organized by a dishwashing detergent manufacturer who claimed that the dirty dishes left by the 16,000 guests could all be washed up using just 1.75 pints/1 liter of their dishwashing liquid.

BIG BRIDGE The successful record attempt was to celebrate the completion of the Vasco da Gama bridge which, back in 1998, was Europe's longest bridge at 10.5 miles/17 km long. So vast was the structure that engineers had to take into account the curvature of the earth! They pulled it off for the princely sum of $1 billion.

The Un-useless Art Of Chindogu

When is an invention useless but also useful? While you scratch your head trying to figure that one out, let's introduce the patron of possibly the world's largest amount of ridiculous objects—Mr. Kenji Kawakami (right). He is the Japanese creator of Chindogu, which, loosely translated, means "un-useless ideas."

These ideas take the form of hundreds of absurd inventions that have become very popular—after all, who couldn't resist the outdoor toilet seat that has a layer of artificial grass to keep your bottom warm? Or perhaps the alarm clock that has sharp pins on the off-button so you never need worry about turning off the alarm and promptly falling back to sleep again?

There is a method to Kenji's madness: He believes at the heart of Chindogu inventions are ideas that (in theory at least) could actually help society and also help us question our views on consumerism. All very worthy. In the meantime, check out the examples of Chindogu on these pages and rate how un-useless-ful you find them.

The Ten Tenets
To ensure that the spirit of Chindogu remains pure, inventor Kenji Kawakami created ten principles that must be adhered to by anyone attempting to create an "unusual implement":

1. A Chindogu cannot be for real use.
2. A Chindogu must exist.
3. Inherent in every Chindogu is the spirit of anarchy.
4. Chindogu are tools for everyday life.
5. Chindogu are not for sale.
6. Humor must not be the sole reason for creating Chindogu.
7. Chindogu are not propaganda.
8. Chindogu are never taboo.
9. Chindogu cannot be patented.
10. Chindogu are without prejudice.

Butterstick

Glue meets butter in this silly but smart idea for saving on cleaning up thanks to the Butter Boy. Dispensed in a glue-applicator-style stick, the butter can be added directly to your toast for the ultimate in laziness. Err, we mean, convenience.

Hay Fever Hat

Pictured right, the user can reach up and pull down some tissue to deal with any errant boogers that may be dangling from the end of their nose. Understandably, you may prefer the idea of having snot all over your face to wearing this contraption.

In this picture (left), Kenji is in his workshop in downtown Tokyo. He proudly displays the prototype for his "two-way shoe," with toes at both ends.

"People need to laugh for no reason...the concept is: You have it, I have it, everybody has this wackiness. This is something that we left behind in our past somehow because of our adulthood, or you're busy doing this or that." Kenji Kawakami, explaining why he continues with the art of Chindogu.

ROTATING SPAGHETTI FORK

It's a hassle having to twirl up spaghetti on your fork—such a hassle, in fact, that Kenji's self-rotating fork is ideal for lazy foodies everywhere. Alas, as the inventor himself confesses, the fork is a perfect example of how Chindogu can solve one problem but lead to a new one: Imagine the spaghetti being rapidly wrapped automatically around the fork for you. Now imagine the pasta covered in Bolognese sauce. Now visualize what your shirt will look like by the end of the meal...we just hope it wasn't white when you started.

Shouting Vase

Angry? Absolutely brain-bendingly furious? Well, a good shout is a great way to unload all that pent-up tension, but suddenly starting to yell at the top of your lungs might scare everyone in your house half to death. So to stop inducing sudden cardiac arrests, we recommend the incredible Shouting Vase, where the user shouts into the opening at the top and the vase muffles the outcry into a whisper, thanks to its soundproofed insides. Genius!

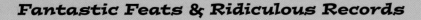

Toilet Special!

You can rent the house for $50,000 a day. That money won't be wasted though—it will be used to aid developing countries.

Living in the Toilet

With house prices going down the toilet, perhaps the toilet-shaped house in South Korea is the perfect symbol for today's housing market. This architectural marvel was built in 2007 to mark the launch of the first general assembly of the World Toilet Association.

The 4,510-square-foot/419-sq-m building made from steel, glass, and white concrete boasts four deluxe toilets—some of them featuring luxury fittings such as electronic motion sensors that detect when your behind is about to descend and lifts and lowers the lid accordingly. Others feature the latest water conservation devices.

The house was built by Sim Jae-duck, who is known in South Korea as Mr. Toilet because of his political work trying to turn public restrooms into pleasant places to be. Indeed, the toilet-shaped house is called Haewoojae, which means "a place of sanctuary where one can solve one's worries."

"The toilet house has become a new cultural icon in the toilet culture movement." The World Toilet Association.

Pass the Paper!

What could be a more fitting addition to the house that's shaped like a toilet? The world's longest toilet roll, of course! Measuring in at a ridiculous 11.4 miles/18.3 km, the toilet roll was unrolled to the world's media back in 2007 in London, England. Weighing a whopping 1,440 pounds/653 kg and boasting a diameter of 5.2 feet/1.6 m, the toilet paper could also be used because it was made by a well-known toilet paper company. It was unrolled from the world's largest toilet-paper-roll holder on the big day, too—another essential purchase for the toilet house above, perhaps!

Lego of My Record!

It often takes a huge amount of effort to create a world record. So you can understand the excitement felt by the folk at Legoland in Windsor, England, when after four days, using 500,000 Lego bricks and the help of a crane, they'd managed to create the world's tallest Lego tower at nearly 97 feet/30 m tall.

Just months later, children in Vienna were amassed as part of the 100 Years of Friends of Children Festival and created their own Lego tower. They beat the tower in Windsor by just a handful of bricks; the Windsor tower stood at 96.1 feet/29.3 m while the one in Vienna (pictured here) was 96.7 feet/29.4 m.

LEGO FACTS It would take 40,000,000,000 Lego bricks to reach the moon. But for those wanting to stay earthbound, they can spend their time working out the 915,103,765 different combinations for combining six eight-stud Lego bricks.

Ross created a plastic model of the intended sculpture before beginning work on the full-sized finished piece of art.

Is It Art?

Or is the astonishing Big Rig Jig sculpture just plain ridiculous? Like the best works from the art world, we think it's a unique combination of both. Created in 2007 by U.S. artist Mike Ross for the popular Burning Man Festival held in the Nevada desert, it featured two full-sized 18-wheeler tanker trucks that towered four stories high. Behind the crazy piece of art is a serious message that has something to do with the global oil industry and the dangerous economic hold it has over our political, social, and environmental systems. Apparently.

"When you stand under it and see a big truck hovering over you, it should give you a sense of danger and fear and that something is wrong." Mike Ross explains the sculpture's message that oil holds a dangerous hold over global society.

STAR ENTRY

Most Ridiculous Object!

Go for a spin on the outrageous bicycles that a mad German has spent most of his adult life creating...

German Dieter "Didi" Senft is a legend in the cycling world for two reasons: first, for his very apparent love of the Tour de France (see box above) and second, because he builds the most crazy bikes on planet Earth. Check out his latest wild creation—the world's biggest mobile guitar (right).

Weighing a hefty half ton, the bike took Didi six months to create and the result is 131 feet/40 m long and 13.8 feet/4.2 m high. To create the bike,

Tour de Farce

When Dieter isn't building a crazy bike with which to astonish the world's media, he can be found following the famous Tour de France cycling competition dressed up as the devil—"El Diablo." Sporting red spandex and horns, he keeps the riders entertained by leaping out and cheering them on. They aren't too surprised by his appearance—he's been turning up at the competition dressed as the devil since 1993 and has a habit of painting a devil's pitchfork on the road several miles before he makes his appearance so the riders have fair warning that they are about to be accosted by the devil!

he used more than 990 feet/300 m of aluminum piping. He also created the remarkable World Cup tricycle (pictured above) that features 100 soccer balls incorporated into its design!

Because of the guitar bike's amazing length, Didi is not allowed to ride the bike on public roads.

BIZARRE BIKES
Didi has built more than 120 cycles and holds multiple world records—from the bike with the smallest front wheel (boasting a diameter of a measly 0.08 inches/2 mm) to the world's longest and largest bike (25.5 feet/7.8 m long and 12 feet/3.7 m high).

That's Just Not Cricket, Old Chap!

Or a hamburger, a racing helmet, a coffee mug, a camera, an eggplant...All of Sudhakar Yadav's creations are in fact cars or bikes. With over 200 built in the shape of everything you could possibly imagine, it was only a matter of time before India-based Sudhakar came up with a cricket-bat car to go with his various sporting-based vehicles (such as a basketball, a football, and a tennis ball) to celebrate and offer support for India in the Cricket World Cup in 2007. Measuring 24.6 feet/7.5 m long, like all of his creations, the crazy motorized bat does actually work on the road!

Sudhakar's creations are massively popular – around 1,000 people visit his museum based in Hyderabad every day.

Sudhakar is planning to create the world's first motorized wildlife park featuring life-sized mechanical animals such as elephants and tigers.

TOP GEAR
Here are some of the details of Sudhakar's incredible creations:

Valentine's Car
Designed for couples on Valentine's Day, this two-seater car adorned with hearts and roses can do 28 mph/ 45 kmh and features suspension, headlights, and indicators.

Potty
The toilet-shaped car features a 50 cc engine and boasts a top speed of 25 mph/40 kmh. The driver sits in the bowl—with the lid up, thankfully.

Tricycle
Sudhakar's world record tricycle is a staggering 41 feet/12.5 m tall, weighs 3 tons, and took three years to build.

WEIRD LOGIC?
So why would you want to go into the world's largest seawater pool when you have the Pacific Ocean right next to it? Well, the water pumped through the artificial lagoon is 9 degrees warmer than the water of the Pacific and has a special filtration system for cleaning the water, too.

Making a Splash

You'd better pack your swim goggles if you're off to the South American resort of San Alfonso del Mar, because even if you want to swim just a single length of its pool, you're in for a half-mile/1-km swim. The world's largest pool took five years to build and cost over a billion dollars, but the result is a spectacular seawater lagoon. It features a 115-foot/35-m deep end—which is about eight times taller than your average three-bedroom house! The water remains so clear at the deep end that you can still see the bottom.

It took 4.4 million pints/2.5 million liters of seawater to fill the pool, which is kept clean in an environmentally friendly way. For those of you who feel slightly tired at the idea of dog paddling your way across such a vast pool, kayaks and sailboats are on hand to whisk guests across it.

The huge pool is equivalent to 6,000 standard swimming pools.

Topsy Turvy World

First, a warning—if you should decide to pay a visit to the remarkable upside-down house on the German island of Usedom, don't try to use the toilet. The reason is simple—everything inside the structure is also upside down. And that includes the chairs, carpets, and toilets.

The house has become something of a hit with tourists as they enter via the attic and then navigate their way around the 1,292-square-foot/120-sq-m family-sized home. The upside-down house is part of a project called Die Welt steht Kopf, which means "The World on Its Head." Other brain-straining exhibits are planned.

Another upside-down house—this time based in Poland—has proved so popular that visitors have been known to wait in line for up to six hours to get inside. But there are reports that visitors can end up feeling seasick. The builders who constructed the house also had to take regular breaks from construction because of feeling disoriented—so the house ended up taking five times longer to build than a normal house.

HEAD OVER HEELS There have been other examples of upside-down houses, but the one in Germany (and another in Poland) are the only ones to feature the entire interior upside down as well. The only thing the right way up is the stairs so visitors can actually move between the floors!

Wheelie Weird

What you are looking at now was seen as a serious transportation solution when it was first proposed back in the late 19th century. Thankfully, the world came to its senses and now the monowheel is seen as something of a dare. Difficult to drive but rewarding (and attention-grabbing) once mastered, the monowheel has become a cult object—and its greatest incarnations have been created by Kerry McLean of Michigan.

His top-of-the-range monowheel is fitted with a Buick V8 engine and has managed speeds of 54 mph/86 kmh so far, though it can, in theory, hit 100 mph/161 kmh. Known as the Rocket Roadster, Kerry also rode it to set the world land speed record for powered single wheelers at the Bonneville Salt Flats in Utah. Be warned though: Although Kerry has spent years mastering the art of building monowheels, it has not been without incident—he once had an accident riding a prototype Rocket Roadster at 50 mph/ 80 kmh...and luckily survived.

McLean's monowheels (he actually refers to them as "monocycles") are available to buy and are fully road legal.

"It's not easy to ride...it's like riding a wheelie the whole time," says Cycleworld's Mark Cernicky.

Off His Rocker

It boasts 50cc of power, can go up to 28 mph/45 kmh, and is totally road legal. Oh, and it's a shopping cart. Hard to believe? Don't worry, you're not alone—the New Zealand police have been trying to get their heads around the contraption as well, pulling over the motorized cart's creator, Duncan Everson, on a regular basis to check that it is fit for the road.

To create his motoring masterpiece, Duncan attached a moped engine to the underside of the cart and fitted the wheels from a lawn mower. He then had it registered for the road and can now be seen whizzing around the roads of Palmerston North, on the North Island of New Zealand.

"I take it out and cruise round The Square on Friday and Saturday nights. I get a few looks!" says Duncan Everson.

Outrageous Risks

We all like to do things that give us a rush—like getting on a roller coaster or being driven in a super-fast car, but for some folk, such pastimes are nowhere near enough...

So you're sitting chatting with your friends and you tell them that you've had a great idea for a stunt. Now imagine telling them that your amazing idea is to fly around London's Big Ben clock tower in an ultralight.

But that's not all; you're going to do it while playing the saxophone. "Um, okay," might be something you hear as your friends try to picture the scene. Then you finish by telling them that you're going to do all of that... while dressed as a gorilla. Cue embarrassed coughs and mumblings

as your friends get up and leave you to think about what you've just said.

But someone has done it—flown an ultralight around Big Ben while dressed as a saxophone-playing gorilla—as you'll see on page 34. Some people are obsessed with taking outrageous risks and are in love with the idea of dazzling their friends and the world with their absurd stunts. This chapter profiles those who have spent their lives searching for the ultimate adrenaline rush. So fasten your seat belts—you're in for a bumpy ride...

Catch the Bus!

Flying through the air for 108 feet/ 33 m over 15 motorbikes while surrounded by a fireball would certainly brighten up that tedious bus journey to school. So if you want a driver qualified enough to make a safe landing as you plummet back down to earth, we recommend hiring Hollywood stuntman Steve Hudis, who pulled off this spectacular stunt—and inadvertently broke a world record for the longest bus jump in the process!

The Qiantang River tidal bore in China (known by locals as the Silver Dragon) is the most notorious in the world—the longest time anyone has managed to surf it is a mere 11 seconds.

The original and greatest daredevil, Evel Knievel, would have approved of Hudis's stunt—Evel usually jumped buses on a bike, though, not the other way around!

Riding the Monster

How would you like picking up your board and waiting for a tidal bore wave to come rushing along a river, bringing everything its swept up along with it? These bizarre waves sweep down rivers at speeds of up to 25 mph/40 kmh and can measure up to 29 feet/9 m in height. They can also cover distances of up to 186 miles/300 km.

The longest nonstop tidal bore surfing record was set by Brazilian Serginho Laus in 2005 when he surfed the Araguari River in Amapa State in his home country. He managed to surf for 6.3 miles/10.1 km for an incredible 33 minutes and 15 seconds!

"The wave is very powerful and can destroy anything—trees, local houses, islands—and sweeps up wild animals." Serginho Laus, on the power of bore waves.

Tidal bores are known as *pororocas* in Brazil, which translates as "monster" or "murderer." Surfing such unpredictable waves is fraught with physical danger—In 2003 Serginho severely injured part of his spine.

STAR ENTRY

Most Outrageous Risk Taker!

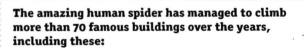

"A city is like a range of mountains, with one little difference—there will always be new skyscrapers under construction." Alain Roberts.

Meet the human spider who climbs up the sides of skyscrapers with no safety equipment—and who suffers from vertigo.

It's called "climbing solo." No, not by yourself because you've got no friends, but climbing without any harnesses, ropes, or other safety gear. It's just you, your wits, and physical dexterity. The master of climbing solo is Frenchman Alain Roberts, who has rightfully earned the nickname Spiderman. He's been climbing unaided since he was a child—his first major achievement was climbing eight floors of the apartment complex he lived in with his parents, because he had forgotten his keys (he was only 12). He has since earned a world record for the most extreme solo route ever climbed, for his ascent up the Gorge of the Verdon, in France.

The amazing human spider has managed to climb more than 70 famous buildings over the years, including these:

Empire State Building	New York	1994
Canary Wharf	London	1995
Golden Gate Bridge	San Francisco	1996
Eiffel Tower	Paris	1996/97
Petronas Twin Towers	Kuala Lumpur	1997
The Sydney Opera House	Australia	1997
Sears Tower	Chicago	1999
Taipei 101	Taiwan	2004

NINE LIVES Two accidents nearly took Alain's life in 1982. The injuries from one of them, after falling 49 feet/15 m head-first, was a five-day coma and fractures of the pelvis, elbows, heels, nose, and cranium. Alain recovered but it left him suffering from vertigo, the condition where you can feel dizzy and unbalanced at great heights. He is now recognized by the French government as being 60 percent disabled because of his condition.

Alain managed to climb only 6.5 feet/2 m of the One Houston Center in Texas before he was grabbed by the police and arrested! He has been arrested on several different occasions while climbing—including during his attempt to climb the New York Times building in Manhattan last year—as he often goes up buildings without authorization from officials!

> If the pilot clips one of the pylons in what the judges consider to be a dangerous maneuver, then he or she can face disqualification.

> The six venues chosen for the 2009 Championship are Abu Dhabi, San Diego, Windsor (Ontario), Budapest, Porto, and Barcelona.

Not Plane Sailing

The Red Bull Air Race World Championship is not for the fainthearted. Hurtling along over land or water approximately 15 feet/4.5 m from the surface while doing 198 mph/320 kmh is considered risky enough by most pilots. Now add in an aerial racetrack that is marked out by air-filled pylons that must be navigated at breakneck speed. All this in front of a crowd of fans quietly thinking that it would be pretty cool to see your plane crash-land (with you miraculously surviving, of course).

Since 2005, the championship has showcased the world's best pilots, racing each other across international cities to win nothing more than prestige. Strapped into planes that can reach up to 229 mph/370 kmh, they race around 3-mile/5-km racetracks, pulling the kind of turns that increases the g force on a pilot's body by a whopping force of 12. Not for the fainthearted.

BUTTER FINGERS The air-filled pylons used to mark out the course may look lethal in the picture here but they have been specially designed to be as safe as possible when hit—which is frequently! Amazingly, when a plane's wing hits the top of a pylon, it simply slices through it "like butter," as one commentator put it. The ground crew then rush out and fix the pylon, filling it back up with air in time for the next race. For those pilots unfortunate enough to clip one of the pylons, a ten-second penalty is added to their final time on completion of the course.

FLY BOY One early morning in London, 1999, commuters would have been amazed to see a ultralight pilot flying under 23 bridges along the river Thames—again, this was the work of the notorious Dangerous Sports Club...

The official mascot of the Dangerous Sports Club is a wheelchair.

Fainthearted Need Not Apply

You might have seen those "crazy guys" on TV throwing themselves into walls, pulling risky pranks, and generally making idiots of themselves, but they are nothing compared with the Dangerous Sports Club. The U.K. club was started in the late '70s by David Kirke, the son of a teacher, and quickly gained risk-loving recruits. The group was the first to make the modern bungee jump; to hang-glide off Mount Kilimanjaro; and to sail across the English Channel tucked into the pouch of an inflatable kangaroo.

Perhaps their greatest achievement was when Alan Weston flew around the Houses of Parliament, in London, wearing a gorilla outfit, playing a saxophone. He was chased by a police helicopter as well as two civilian helicopters. Upon landing, the group quickly bundled Weston into a car and put him on the first plane back to America. Why America? Oh yes, Weston is a rocket scientist for the U.S. Air Force.

> *"I crossed the Channel in it. A jumbo pilot saw me at 100 feet and assumed it was a UFO."* David Kirke on crossing the English Channel in the pouch of a giant helium-filled kangaroo.

When Risks Go Wrong

Back in 2000, Stella Young was launched 69 feet/21 m into the air from a medieval-style catapult. She traveled at 50 mph/80 kmh before coming back down to earth. Sadly, when she hit the safety net, she bounced out of it and fell to the ground, fracturing her pelvis.

In 2002 though, things turned far more serious when a member of the club was killed after being thrown 98 feet/30 m into the air by the very same device (above).

There are many rules to be followed during the run—one of which is that if you do fall down, don't under any circumstances try to get back up immediately. Instead, stay down, cover your head, and hope that you only get bruised as the bulls rush over you…

PLAYING CHICKEN Runners who try to climb their way out of trouble could find themselves being pushed off any safe perch by onlookers. And if you think rushing ahead of the bulls will keep you safe, you're right—but you face public humiliation as you run into the Plaza del Toros, the final destination of the bull run, because the crowds will boo and hiss at you for being a such a chicken!

Run for Your Life!

It is believed that 15 people have died during the bull run and over 200 have suffered serious injuries.

Just a quick word to the wise—if you should find yourself on the streets of the Spanish city of Pamplona between July 7–14 at 8 A.M., you might want to hide. Quickly. If not, you're about to become involved in the extremely dangerous tradition of the running of the bulls, part of the Festival of San Fermin. This controversial custom sees everyone dressed in white with red neckerchiefs, trying to outrun six fighting bulls plus two herds of bullocks along a 2,706-foot/825-m course. Now, it may take only three minutes to complete, but that's long enough to be trampled under hoof by a bull or have one of their horns catch you in the chest with sometimes fatal consequences.

The route is laid out by erecting double-lined fences along the streets of Pamplona. There is a gap between the two fences where medical teams stand, ready to try to rescue any participant who gets mown down by one of the bulls.

To Infinity and Beyond!

It may look like something out of *James Bond*, but the man strapped into this jet-powered wing is no special effect—he is 49-year-old Yves Rossy, who broke the world record for being the first man to fly solo across the English Channel from Calais to Dover using a jet-propelled wing. With the giant wing strapped to his back, Yves made the 22-mile/35.4-km flight in 9 minutes and 7 seconds, traveling at an average speed of 124 mph/200 kmh. Amazingly, Yves built this record-breaking, four-jet engine in his garage!

It is believed that Yves will attempt to fly through the Grand Canyon in the U.S. for his next jet-powered challenge.

When not breaking records, Yves used to fly Mirage fighters for the Swiss army and is now an airline pilot. In his downtime, he likes to parachute—he's done 1,100 jumps so far!

> **"I fuse with my machine. It was my dream as a boy to be a bird."**
> Yves Rossy explained his passion for flying before his record-breaking Channel-crossing attempt.

Markus beat the eight-year-old previous world record by 14 mph/22.5 kmh. And guess who set that previous world record? Why, Markus of course!

Snow Fear

It's not surprising that Austrian Markus Stoeckl is known as "Hercules." Although that nickname is attributed to his 6.2-foot/190-cm height, we reckon it should be because of his complete lack of fear. After all, here is the guy who smashed the existing world speed record for series mountain bikes by shooting down the snow-covered, 45-degree, 6,560-foot/2,000-m La Parva slope in Chile, hitting a top speed of 210.4 mph/338.7 kmh. It took him only 40 seconds to complete the high-speed run, which was lucky, because he had to hold his breath while breaking the record, or else his special aerodynamic helmet would have steamed up because of his warm breath.

> **"I was very calm. At the end of the course, I had the feeling that I was watching myself riding."**
> Markus Stoeckl on breaking his mountain-biking world record.

Man at Work

Brit Thomas Blackthorne is a man of many bizarre hobbies—for instance, he eats glass, shampoo, and razor blades and enjoys sleeping in pits of snakes. He's also partial to walking on sword blades and through acid baths. And in his downtime, you'll probably find him studying languages—he is already fluent in three.

Thomas has also set other world records, including the heaviest tongue lift, where he lifted 26 pounds/12 kg of pasta in a glass-walled box, using just his tongue.

But perhaps the most spectacular feat Blackthorne has pulled off was appearing on German TV in 2007 and proceeding to push the 1-inch/25-mm bit of a demolition hammer down his throat and holding it—and the entire weight of the hammer—for three seconds all on his own. This incredible act of daring (and insanity) earned him a record for the heaviest object to be sword-swallowed. It took three attempts before he managed to push the oil-drenched hammer bit down his throat—much to the audience's discomfort!

HEAVY, MAN It's worth remembering that the demolition hammer's weight was 84 pounds/38 kg, which is about half the weight of a grown man. To get the demolition hammer up in the air to shoulder height, it had to be hoisted up via a motorized chain. From there, Thomas had to lift the jackhammer himself, position it over his mouth, and then guide it down his throat. To finish off, he rested the entire weight of the demolition hammer on his upper lip and teeth for those three long and tortuous seconds...

Ted says that when he was younger, if he was talking to a girl at a party who wasn't very interested in him, he would dive through the nearest window to get her full, undivided attention!

Man on Fire

Not many people fancy the idea of being flame-grilled, but for stuntman and daredevil Ted Batchelor, no fire is too scorching. He's already set the record for the longest full-body burn without an oxygen supply in 2004—he managed to stay alight (and alive) for 2 minutes and 38 seconds—but his passion for fiery death-defying feats doesn't stop there. Ted's favorite stunt is to set himself on fire, then after walking around for a minute, throw himself off the Chagrin Falls in Ohio to extinguish himself. The first time he did the stunt was back in 1976 when he was trying to win a bet as a student. Then throughout the late '70s and early '80s, he repeated the same feat—trouble was, the authorities weren't happy and he's already been fined, locked up for days at a time, and put on probation. Thankfully, the local authorities have finally given him their consent so Ted the human fireball can dive off the falls to his heart's content.

WARNING! Although Ted loves his work with fire, he doesn't encourage anyone to follow in his footsteps—including his two children. Ted says that he has been burned throughout his career and what he does is always fraught with danger. Do not try this at home.

Head Over Heels!

> Travis practiced for his double backflip more than 1,000 times in a special foam pit he has at home.

The world of motorcycling was turned upside down on August 4, 2006. Well, turned upside down twice. Backward, in fact. The motocross world's biggest hero, Travis Pastrana, managed to perform the world's first freestyle motocross double backflip in the fearsome X Games. The amazing feat also landed him the highest score ever given by the judges at the Best Trick event; not surprising, really, when you consider how dangerous the stunt was—landing wrongly could have at best destroyed his career through injury and at worst killed him.

Flipping 720 degrees also requires more height than the usual flip, and as Travis himself noted in his book, *The Big Jump*, he only realized during the jump itself how perilously close he came to hitting one of the big spotlights hanging above the ramp course. If he had hit it, he would have fallen 49 feet/15 m to the ground. In the meantime, Travis has stated that he will not be attempting another double backflip—he reckons it's up to others to follow in his tire marks!

> *"What inspires me and motivates me is someone saying that something can't be done. Or someone saying that you're not good enough.*
> Travis Pastrana.

> Travis wasn't sure if he should go ahead with the daring double backflip right up until the last minute—he let a game of rock, paper, scissors make the decision for him.

STUNT JUNKIE! In his downtime, Travis also enjoys skydiving—without a parachute! In September 2008, he leaped from a plane at 12,500 feet/3,810 m without one and had to glide his way to his jump partner, who grabbed his hands. He pulled himself onto his fellow skydiver's back before his partner's parachute cord was pulled!

The Lion King

Lions: big, pointy teeth, known for biting and eating people. Children: like playing soccer and Playstation, and eating sugary snacks. You wouldn't have thought the two would mix, but then you would be wrong. Pictured here is the world's youngest lion tamer, Jorge Elich, an eight-year-old who has become such an expert that he now practices his deadly art at the Circus Paris in El Ejido in Spain. His gift for staring into the jaws of death and then telling them to behave is not something new to him. The youngest of his six brothers and sisters, he actually started taming lions when he was just five years old; the reason for this remarkable education is because of his lion-taming dad, who has become increasingly weak over the years and the family needed to step in and help out. We think he's gone above and beyond the call of duty!

The Wheel Deal

"Hardcore sitting" is the label 16-year-old Aaron "Wheels" Fotheringham has given to the extreme stunts he pulls in his wheelchair at a skateboard park in Las Vegas, Nevada. It involves pulling the kind of feats and tricks that would leave a pro skateboarder looking tame, and Aaron is so good at it that he landed himself a world record for performing the first ever backflip in a wheelchair. The chair is made from aluminum for lightness and strength, has special suspension to take the impact of the landings, and features "grind bars" that help Aaron achieve his amazing stunts.

The amazing Aaron started using a wheelchair when he was just three and has been using it full-time since he was eight—he suffers from a genetic condition known as spina bifida.

"Being in a wheelchair is like carrying your skateboard with you," explains Aaron.

Buried Alive!

Well, it's one way of whiling away the days—being buried alive in a 6.8-foot/2.1-m-long wooden box. Geoff Smith of Mansfield, England, was buried 5.9 feet/1.8 m under the garden of his local pub, the Railway Inn, in 1999. He managed to stay down there for a record-breaking 147 days, breathing through a 9-inch/23-cm-wide tube that was also used to pass food down to him and for the removal of body waste. Here's hoping they washed the tube on a regular basis...

For company, Geoff had a small television, a personal stereo, a cell phone, and a small Christmas tree—yes, he ended up spending Christmas buried alive as well! Geoff wanted to bury himself alive in tribute to his late mother, Emma, who clearly wasn't claustrophobic either—in 1968, she set the original world record of 101 days. This was topped in 1981 by an American who managed a crazy 141 days.

The record for the most time spent buried alive without food or water belongs to Zdenek Zahradka, who spent 10 days buried in a wooden coffin in Jaromer, Czech Republic, in 2004. The previous record stood at four days.

"When his mother did it, he [Geoff] was seven years old. He's now 37 and for the last 30 years, it's been his ambition to go and bury himself in a box."
Hartley Hughes, pub landlord of the Railway Inn.

Shocked by the Block!

So he's a super-successful rally driver. He's also a co-founder of a booming shoe business. But that all pales in comparison with what Ken Block does in his spare time for kicks—he loves to go jumping in his Subaru Impreza WRX STi. His most incredible achievement was in 2007 at the New Zealand Snow Park. After fitting his Impreza with special snow tires, he pulled off one of the most amazing feats ever attempted by a driver, by making a huge 68-foot/21-m jump in sync with a pro snowboarder.

"I know the physics: 90 miles per hour through trees sideways is pretty damn scary." Ken Block on the danger involved in performing his snow stunt.

In New Zealand, Ken attempted another jump that was less successful—he overshot the landing ramp and wrote off the Subaru as he landed nose-first into flat ground. Ken later found out that he had cracked one of his vertebrae in the process.

Peculiar People

Some people are born a bit different, others spend a lifetime trying to get themselves noticed. Whatever the case, the world is full of peculiar but amazing people...

It can be difficult when you stand out from the crowd. It might be because you're really big or teeny tiny; perhaps you have big ears or hair growing out of odd places. You may feel a little shy about going out in public but you shouldn't!

Take a tip from the following amazing folk who are blessed with truly unique looks or bodies. They certainly aren't ashamed of it—either through choice or through nature, they're living with what they have, celebrating it, and most important, letting the world know about it.

Some turn it into an artform, like the mad moustached fellow on page 47. Others show themselves to the world in the hope that we will better understand their conditions—read about brave Dede "Tree Man" Koswara on page 46 and the Gomez family on page 49.

This chapter is dedicated to these fearless folk, and we'll take you around the world looking at some of the amazing attributes of the world's most phenomenal people.

Body Beautiful?

You would have thought that Australian Ray Moon might have decided to take it easy at the ripe old age of 79. After all, here is a man who has had open-heart surgery, overcome polio, been fitted with a pacemaker, suffered prostate problems, oh, and was pronounced clinically dead on one occasion.

But showing true Aussie grit, Ray decided to walk right past the golf course, turned his nose up at playing cards with other senior citizens, and instead, for the past four years, has been working out for two and a half hours a day up to six days a week to get himself into the kind of shape that men half his age would kill for.

Because of his punishing workout routine, Ray has become what many believe is the world's oldest bodybuilder by winning the over-60s division of the Victorian Bodybuilding Championships in Melbourne in September 2008.

Ray used to be a millionaire chef and restaurateur and has cooked for the Queen of England! But his business folded and he lost everything. Getting into such fine shape was his way of dealing with the failure.

Before her death in early 2008, Morjorie Newlin became a national celebrity in the U.S., appearing on shows such as *Oprah*. Why? Because of her bodybuilding work—she worked out daily for more than 15 years and was pumping iron until the ripe old age of 87.

"I train five days a week, two hours on exercises and cardio and I also walk three or four kilometers a day on the treadmill."
Ray Moon on his workout regimen.

The Eating Machine

It took two years for the incredible Frenchman Michel Lotito to eat his way through a Cessna 150 aeroplane between 1978 and 1980. It was a stunt that earned him not only a world record but also brought him to the attention of the world's media. Dubbed "Monsieur Mangetout," he went on to shock people with his unorthodox appetite for anything that didn't contain vitamins—including 18 bicycles, seven televisions, two beds, and an entire coffin.

His amazing ability to munch up to 1.8 pounds/900 g of metal every day was put down to his stomach lining being twice the thickness of a normal person's. Oh, and a whole lot of practice, too—he started eating metal at the age of nine. And no, we don't recommend that you try to eat your stereo to see if your stomach lining is as thick as Monsieur Mangetout's...

Mr. Mangetout died in 2006 of non-metal-eating-related causes.

"We've tried to understand this phenomenon, these antidotes created by his body, but he's basically a normal guy," *explains Dr. Bernard Morzol, who studied the incredible Monsieur Mangetout when he was alive.*

To help you grow up big and strong, it has always been recommended that you have three proper meals a day.

Now, to ensure that this common-sense advice meets the recommended minimum ridiculous quota for this book, we present here the perfect menu for those wanting to have their three-meals-a-day while remaining utterly mad:

Stuff-Your-Face Special

Breakfast

For breakfast, you could follow in the footsteps of Luppan Yau, who managed to polish off five and a half breakfasts at the 2007 All You Can Eat Breakfast Eating Championships in London, England. The meal included eggs, bacon, sausage, mushrooms, and croissant, and Luppan wolfed it all down in an amazing 12 minutes. You shouldn't be surprised though, because he had previously set a record for eating the most doughnuts in three minutes.

Lunch

For lunch, head to the Wing Bowl competition in San Jose, California, where competitors fight to eat as many buffalo wings as possible. You may have a hard time beating Joey Chestnut, though, who in 2008 managed to eat 241 buffalo wings, winning a Harley Davidson and a new pickup truck! He didn't feel nervous even with 20,000 people watching.

A word of warning—if you eat like this on a regular basis, you could end up like the guy on page 44.

Dinner

For dinner, we recommend the fine haute cuisine dish of hot dog at Nathan's Famous July Fourth International Hot Dog Eating Contest in New York. You're likely to face some stiff competition from a familiar face, though. Yes, the winner of the Wing Bowl, Joey Chestnut, has been munching his way across the U.S. and holds several world records for his eating antics—in this case, consuming 66 hot dogs in just 12 minutes in 2007. He was nearly beaten the following year when he went up against Takeru "Tsunami" Kobayashi— they both managed to eat exactly 59 hot dogs before Joey stuffed his face to victory in a five-hot dog face-off.

"I didn't grow up wanting to do this at all. It's something that chose me."
Joey Chestnut about what drives him to eat for fame.

The Human Pincushion

Brazilian-born Elaine Davidson is the current world record holder for being the most pierced woman on the planet. The former nurse, who now lives in Edinburgh, Scotland, was first spotted when she sported 462 piercings (with 192 of those being on her face). Fast-forward to today, and she now has more than 4,000. Elaine has calculated that all her studs and rings together weigh a whopping 6.6 pounds/3 kg—that's the same weight as carrying around two whole chickens all the time.

"People often just want to look at me or touch me—some even want to kiss me!"
Elaine explains people's reactions to her piercings.

SPEED PIERCING The current record for the most piercings ever made in a single session is 1,015. The record was set by UK-based Charlie Wilson and Kam Ma in March 2006. It took seven hours and 55 minutes for all the piercings to be made. That's a very long time to say "oooouuuuch"...

Three Baby Elephants...

... That's the equivalent of how much Mexican Manuel Uribe weighed back in 2006—an immense 1,232 pounds/560 kg—which made him what many believed to be the world's heaviest man. He began to pile on the weight soon after he moved to the U.S. to work as a computer repairman in 1988. Trouble was, in between fixing PCs, he constantly ate pizza, tacos, and burgers, and eventually ballooned to the weight of a small hatchback car!

But not anymore—now back in Mexico, Manuel has been on a strict diet and has lost 561 pounds/255 kg. It's a far cry from his earlier years when he was confined to his bed, leaving his house only three times in six years. The reason for his weight loss? A beautiful woman, of course. It was Manuel's wish to walk girlfriend Claudia Solis down the aisle, unaided, which he proudly achieved in 2008.

Manuel's new diet consists of five meals a day—a typical meal is fish soup, some fruit, and 18 peanuts.

"I have a wife and will form a new family and live a happy life," *Manuel Uribe told reporters on his supersized wedding day.*

A Tall Story

Measuring in at a whopping 7 feet, 9 inches/2.3 m, 59-year-old Mongolian Bao Xishun never has to worry about reaching the top shelf in the supermarket. Being officially the world's tallest man, he quite literally has the world at his fingertips.

As you might imagine, life hasn't always been easy for the gentle giant— although he is lucky to be in good health, for many years he found it difficult to find love. An international appeal was set up to find the towering man a suitable bride, but after all the media attention, he actually managed to find love far closer to home than he could have hoped for in the shape of a saleswoman from his hometown, Chifeng. They tied the knot in 2007 and are now the proud parents of an only-just-slightly-bigger-than-average baby boy. A tall story with a very happy ending.

The tallest man to ever have lived was American Robert Walow—when he died in 1940, Robert measured an astonishing 9 feet, 11 inches/2.72 m.

Bao is famous for more than just his height—he hit headlines in 2006 when he saved two dolphins in China thanks to his incredibly long arms. The dolphins had swallowed plastic and experts had been unable to remove it. Enter Mr. Bao, who was able to gently insert his hands into the dolphins' mouths, reach into their stomachs, and take out the plastic.

TALL ORDER Bao was first crowned the world's tallest man in 2006. However, in 2007 the honor fell upon Ukranian Leonid Stadnyk, who measured 8 feet, 5.5 inches/ 2.57 m. Record officials needed to measure Leonid again in order for him to retain his title, but he refused, so the record was returned to Bao in 2008 . Interestingly, Leonid Stadnyk's height is attributed to a condition known as *acromegalic gigantism*, whereas Bao is believed to be naturally tall.

The Tree Man

It began with a single small wart on Dede Koswara's lower leg when he was 15 years old. Trouble was, the wart then proceeded to spread all over his body. By the time the man from West Java, Indonesia, came to the attention of the media, his hands and feet were covered in huge clumps of warts that looked like tree bark. The rest of his body was badly affected as well.

After he became known as "The Tree Man of Java," experts rushed to see exactly what was causing the huge and unsightly growths that had changed Dede's life and discovered that he had a rare condition that kept his body from fighting off warts. To make matters worse, X rays revealed that because of his condition, Dede had also contracted deadly tuberculosis, which his body couldn't fight off. Thankfully, he has received treatment that has cured the tuberculosis and surgeons have performed four operations so far on his growths—one operation saw them remove a staggering 4.4 pounds/2 kg of warts from his hands and feet.

The bizarre wart growths are known as "cutaneous horns."

Thanks to the operations, Dede has been able to use his hands again for the first time in more than ten years.

"The first priority is to get cured and get a job, but as a father, of course I want my son to remarry. He is a normal guy and he is still a young man." Ateng Koswara, on his son's condition.

The Queen of Corsets...

... is how Cathie Jung is known to some because she has the world's smallest waist, measuring a teeny tiny 15 inches/38.1 cm. To achieve this amazing waist, Cathie has not gone under the knife or been on any special diets. Nope, she's managed to pull it off by wearing corsets pulled very tight day and night for more than 25 years. The 71-year-old American woman is married to an orthopedic surgeon, who believes Cathie's love of corset wearing does her no harm and could actually help support her spine, not damage it.

The Queen of Corsets owns more than 100 of the traditional ladies' undergarments.

Cathie Jung's idol is the now deceased Ethel Granger, a British woman, who had a waist that measured only 13 inches/33 cm—the smallest waist ever officially recorded.

"I always liked corsets. When I watched films like Gone with the Wind *and* Seven Brides for Seven Brothers, *I just loved the women's figures,"* Cathie Jung explains.

STAR ENTRY

Most Peculiar People

Meet the bearded wonders of the world who love to show off their wacky whiskers...

These fine purveyors of facial fur meet once every two years to beard-off at the largest competition of its type, the World Beard and Moustache Championships. The year 2007 saw 252 entries descend on the seaside resort of Brighton, England, to battle it out in three categories.

These categories are Moustache, Partial Beard, and Full Beard, and within these, there are several classes. For instance, the classes within Partial Beard are natural goatee, Chinese, Musketeer, Imperial, Partial Beard Freestyle, and the dramatic Sideburns Freestyle class. Unsurprisingly, the Freestyle classes are the most popular and contestants have been known to go to great lengths to impress the judges—one competitor at the Berlin event in 2005 used his beard to re-create the city's famous and iconic landmark, the Brandenburg Gate, which included horses and flags!

The Hair Pretzel
Pictured here is Willi Chevalier from Germany, who won the Partial Beard Freestyle category in 2007. Willi has been a regular winner in the Partial Beard Freestyle class—the only time he missed out on victory was at the 2003 Championships because, according to officials, he had "an unfortunate encounter with a power drill."

MAD ABOUT BEARDS
The 2007 championships were boycotted by members of the Beard Liberation Front because they felt that the competitors were spending far too much time looking after their facial hair. Its organizer, Keith Flett (who is also the spokesperson for the Campaign for Real Conkers) believes that fussing too much over your facial hair is having a negative impact on sporting a beard in public!

The rules state that no hair extensions, false facial hair, unnatural hair color or hairpins are allowed.

Georges doesn't know his own strength sometimes—at a motor show, he accidentally managed to remove the entire bumper off a car he was admiring!

Georges enjoys blowing up hot water bottles, too—it takes him 40 seconds to inflate one with his breath before it pops. He has to be extremely careful, though, because if he allowed the air he'd blown into the bottle to rush back out and back into his lungs, his lungs would explode!

Just Plane Mad

Frenchman Georges Christen boasts a series of biceps-rippling achievements. He's ripped up 23 telephone directories in two minutes, bent 269 nails in a single hour, pulled a 22-ton railroad car 328 feet/100 m, carried a woman perched on a table with his teeth for 32 feet/10 m, and much, much more. In fact, he claims to have set more than 20 world records!

Perhaps his most impressive feat was back in 1990 when the record breaker stopped three 110-hp Cessna aircraft from taking off, using his arms to stop two of them moving and using his teeth to stop the third. It's all the more impressive because the planes' engines were cranked up to full power at the time!

Georges regularly tours the world with his PowerShow display.

"I always wanted to perform like [those] old strongmen which I loved as a kid. I wanted to be the person the kids were amazed at," Georges Christen explains.

He's So Licky!

The female with the longest tongue in the world is German teenager Annika Irmler, whose tongue measures 2.7 inches/ 7 cm.

Stephen Taylor, a teaching assistant from Coventry in Britain, likes nothing more than sticking his tongue out. After all, it's made him famous because it is officially recognized as the world's biggest—measuring 3.7 inches/9.5 cm from the middle of his closed lip to the very tip of his tongue.

His tongue also helped win the heart of his partner, Rachel Evans, who, on seeing the titanic tongue, burst out laughing. There is a downside, though— she worries that she may be suffocated by his huge tongue when they kiss. Gross!

WHAT A MOUTHFUL Stephen claims that his tongue is continuing to grow—he reckons it's now 4 inches/10 cm. He is concerned that if it keeps growing, his tongue will no longer fit in his mouth. Surely that's another world record in the making...

Hair-Raising Family

The Gomez family is a remarkable one—many family members suffer from a condition known as "hypertrichosis," which means that they have thick hair all over their bodies. Pictured here is Danny Ramos Gomez, who performs as an acrobat alongside his brother, Larry, for the Mexican National Circus. Because of their condition they had a difficult start in life—they spent their childhood as part of a freak show where they were called the "wolf children" and spent their time sitting in a cage for passersby to laugh at. Thankfully, they were rescued by the son of a circus owner and have been trained in many different performing arts.

KEEPING IT IN THE FAMILY There are around 20 Gomez family members who have the condition—that's at least five generations. Some, though, have not been affected, such as Danny's grandmother, but she does have the gene that was passed on to her children. According to research carried out on the family by geneticist Dr. Luis Figuera, the women in the family have a 50 percent chance of passing the gene on to their children, whereas the men in the family can't pass it on to their sons but are guaranteed to pass it on to their daughters.

"I'd never take it off. I'm very proud to be who I am," said Larry Ramos Gomez, about the hair on his body, for which there is no treatment.

Bendy Boy

From a distance, the amazing antics of seven-year-old Indian lad Aniket Chindak are akin to a pond skater that skims gracefully along the surface of water—except Aniket shoots across tarmac on skates and under cars. He has managed to limbo-skate under 82 cars in just 53 seconds so far. It's no easy task either—to keep himself fit for such feats, Aniket currently trains up to four hours a day, sometimes covering as much as 60 miles/97 km in a single week. We shouldn't be too surprised, though, because he's been obsessed with skating since he was only 18 months old!

When Aniket is limbo-skating, his body is never more than 8 inches/ 20 cm above the ground.

Aniket is now in training to limbo-skate under an astonishing 100 cars.

"It took three months before I could get my body in the right position. Since then I have skated under lots of cars and have never hurt myself. The hardest thing is to go fast enough before I bend down. That's how you can skate under so many cars at once," Aniket Chindak explains to The New Indian Express newspaper.

Good Things Come in Small Packages

He's only the size of a six-month-old baby, but 20-year-old He Pingping makes a very big impression on all those he meets. Since being discovered, the 2 foot, 5.37-inch/73-cm Mongolian man (who has been declared the world's shortest mobile man) has become something of a jet-setter as the world has clamored to meet him. The wee man was born with primordial dwarfism and, according to his father, could fit into the palm of his hand when he was born.

Pingping lives only 805 km/500 miles away from the world's tallest man—fellow Mongolian, Bao Xishun (see page 45).

The world's shortest mobile man has special features in his home to help with his height—his doorknobs are lowered, and when he sits down to dinner, he uses a high chair.

DEFINITION OF MOBILE The reason he is recorded as the world's shortest "mobile" man is because there are actually shorter people out there—the shortest man in the world is Lin Yih-Chih, who measures in at a tiny 27 inches/67.5 cm, and the world's shortest woman is Madge Bester, at 2 feet, 1.5 inches/65 cm. However, they both have to use wheelchairs because of a rare medical condition.

Eye Karumba!

It has to be one of the most disturbing sights recorded yet—an apparently normal-looking person who can pop their eyeballs out from their eye sockets so far that they look like a cartoon character. American Kim Goodman is one such "eye popper" and in 2007 her protruding eyes were measured at 0.47 inches/12 mm.

Popping your eyeballs strains blood vessels and nerves that attach your eyes to your head. In theory, though, being able to pop your eyes won't cause you any harm. But still, best not to give it a try—would you really want Kim's ability?

EYE TO EYE Brazilian Claudio Paulo Pinto reckons that his eye-popping abilities are catching up with Kim's. A former haunted house employee whose job was to scare visitors, Claudio's eye-popping has been measured at 0.27 inches/7mm. Claudio reckons that his eye-popping abilities have increased by over 50 percent, so Kim may need to keep an eye out for him...

Wim's next world record-breaking attempt will be to sit in a container filled with ice for 1 hour and 41 minutes!

Ice Work if You Can Get It!

How do you like the idea of ascending Mount Everest in nothing but your undies? Or chilling out in a container of ice for over an hour? Or perhaps doing a half marathon barefoot several miles north of the Arctic Circle? If that sounds like your idea of hell (frozen over), then pity Wim Hof, aka the Ice Man, a Dutchman who is able to withstand the kind of temperatures that would prove fatal for the rest of us. Wim reckons that his ability to withstand such extreme icy conditions is because of a form of Himalayan meditation he practices, called Tummo, which he claims can help him generate heat in any part of his body.

"My goggles froze and I lost the track and so I went off course a little...a diver gripped my almost-unconscious body, and drew me back to the 60-meter hole." Wim "Ice Man" Hof about his record-breaking swim under ice at the North Pole in 2002, which saw him miss the exit hole carved out in the ice.

Making a Big Splash

We all know just how painful it can be to belly-flop into a swimming pool. Now imagine what it must be like for Darren Taylor, aka Professor Splash from Denver, Colorado, who regularly sets world records for the highest shallow diving. His latest record-breaking feat saw him dive from a height of 35 feet/10.7 m into a mere 12 inches/30.5 cm of water, in 2008.

"Kids will usually wander around after a dive show and just walk right up and say, 'I wanted to see you land flat.'" Darren Taylor writes about the dangers of shallow diving.

Stretching Your Disbelief!

Although Gary "Stretch" Turner looks like he is wearing some kind of prosthetic face and is ready to walk onto the set of a horror film, that flappy skin is for real. Because of Ehlers-Danlos syndrome, a condition that has left Gary's skin incredibly thin, he is able to pull out his skin as if it is elasticized. Holder of the world record for the planet's most stretchy skin, Gary now tours with the Circus of Horrors, bedazzling and shocking audiences with his skin-stretching antics, which can see him pulling up his neck skin to cover his entire mouth. Lovely.

Gary also holds the world record for the most clothespins attached to a person's face—he managed a staggering 159 in 2004.

"I am proud of being called a freak. I think of all the great performers that have gone before. It is an honor," says Gary Turner of his "freak" status.

A HIGH PRICE It's not all good for our Gary—he needs painkillers to help deal with the pain he has in his joints because of his condition; stretching his skin does not hurt him, thankfully.

The Cat Man

What would you do to make yourself look like a cat? Well, a pair of fake whiskers wasn't enough for Dennis Avner—he's had surgery to flatten and upturn his nose, had his teeth removed and tiger-like fangs inserted in their place, had brow implants fitted; had his body covered in striped tiger tattoos, and even had his ears lengthened. To top all that off, Dennis has also had receptacles fitted to his upper lip—these mean he can attach proper whiskers on special occasions.

Oh, and his name is no longer Dennis—it's now Stalking Cat. Mr. Cat began making the changes to his body when he was 23 years old because of his upbringing in a Native American community. It inspired him to take on the appearance of his totem symbol, that of a tiger. Oh, and when he's not amazing people with his looks, he fixes computers!

Stalking Cat is officially the world's most modified man.

"I eat meat every day, just as a tiger would. It must be as close to raw as possible, or at the temperature that an animal would be if it had just been killed." *Stalking Cat talks to* The Sun *newspaper about his special diet.*

Preposterous Pastimes

The world is filled with different creeds, colors, and cultures. But we're all the same when you get down to it—we all love having fun and laughing at our own ridiculousness; it's tradition, see...

Whether it's hundreds of people in a Thai town squirting each other with water pistols or folk snorkeling in a freezing bog in Wales, preposterous pastimes are the best way for people to bond and to laugh at the event itself and, more importantly, at each other. In a good-natured way, of course.

What really makes these pastimes so much fun is that you are free to be extremely mischievous and do things that would normally be followed by frowns of disapproval. There's no time for such tellings-off from stern types during these events, though, because they're way too busy themselves getting pelted with tomatoes (see page 60) or dressing up as ninjas (see page 56).

So enjoy the freedom over the next few pages and be inspired; perhaps you too can dream up a devilish pursuit that could one day be passed off as a preposterous pastime...

Peat Up or Bog Off!

Best not to get too bogged down with detail on this particular preposterous pastime – after all, the premise is simple enough. Two 180-foot/55-m trenches are dug out in the Waen Rhydd Bog just outside Britain's smallest town, Llanwrtyf Wells in Wales, during the month of August. Contestants are then required to swim down the trench wearing flippers and a snorkel, and whoever does it in the fastest time is declared the winner.

The water has been described as having the consistency of pea soup; its smell could be tastefully described as being a bit pungent (and tastes even worse, sometimes providing the swimmers with a snack in the shape of a newt); and, if you're not wearing a wet suit, you can expect to find the water somewhat chilly. The event has been going for over 20 years now and keeps on attracting people who gladly put themselves through such trench warfare all in the name of a local charity. So it's worth the suffering and humiliation. Just.

Bog-snorkeling participants do not use regular swimming techniques to make it down the trenches—that would be too easy (and make them look normal).

Bored with your flippers? Sick of sucking up rancid water? Then why not try the Mountain Bike Snorkeling Championship!

Gurn and Bear It

What is gurning and why do people do it? The answer to the former is the art of making faces; the answer to the latter is unknown. What we do know is that Tommy "Quasimodo" Mattinson, a 41-year-old Briton, has won the World Gurning Championship 11 times and has earned himself a place in the record books.

Held at the Egremont Crab Fair in Cumbria, England, the gurning championship is world famous for featuring people putting their heads through a horse collar and proceeding to scrunch up their faces into the most hideous poses imaginable. Tommy has staved off some fierce (and seriously ugly) competition over the years to claim his hard-won record.

Mattinson's facial exploits were witnessed by the Queen during a visit she made to Cumbria to celebrate the 300th anniversary of a town in the area. She was mildly amused.

"Don't stay like that for too long or your face will stay like that." Prince Philip to Tommy Mattinson, the Gurning World Champion.

THE FAIRER SEX? 60-year-old Anne Woods' gurning is arguably even more impressive than Tommy's facial antics. She has been gurning "competitively" now for 31 years and has won the Ladies' Gurning Championship a staggering 20 times. Anne's success could well be attributed to her being able to remove her dentures, making her wrinkled face as ugly as a squashed prune.

Being shot out of a cannon at 59 mph/96 kmh is no walk in the park. David Smith Jr. has broken a leg, and his sister, Stephanie, once suffered spinal injuries after her landing in the safety airbag went wrong.

The Cannonball Family

It must make for an interesting discussion when sitting around the family dinner table: "Son, what are you doing today?" "Well, I'm firing myself out of a cannon. And my sister is too. And my cousin. We're all following in your scorched footsteps, Dad." Meet the Smith family, who have been firing themselves out of cannons for decades.

First, it was David "Cannonball" Smith Sr., who made his name by setting the world record for the farthest human cannonball flight at 184 feet/56 m in 1998. Then, his son, David "The Bullet" Smith Jr., stepped in, followed by his sister, Stephanie, and one of their cousins. Together, they have the human cannonball act pretty much sewn up.

David Smith Sr. still enjoys the odd blast (in between making and maintaining cannons for his family members) and has traveled the world entertaining the crowds. He even made his flying an art form when he was shot over the Mexican/U.S. border in 2005 as part of an art exhibit.

Pity poor Todd Christian, who was a fearless human cannonball right up until the moment he was fired in 2005 for refusing to go on a special training course in Brazil. The reason? He is afraid of flying over long distances...

MEAN FEAT OF PHYSICS It's a dangerous job being a human cannonball and one that requires careful planning—calculations have to be made to ensure that you land in the safety net 147 feet/45 m away, and the wind, distance, and height must be considered. Once you're happy with the calculations, you can then be fired out of the cannon—but you must keep your body straight at all times when in the cannon so your trajectory is not off once you're launched. As you're fired out, you can expect to experience a g force of 11—that's 11 times your body weight.

Ninja fact: A few hundred ninjas managed to wipe out 10,000 samurai in a fierce battle in 1580.

Ninja fact: It is said that one ninja faked his own death so that when he was seen again, people thought that his ghost had come back from beyond the grave.

Meet the Ninjas

Ninja fact: When going to sleep, ninjas would always rest on their left side to protect their hearts from a sudden knife attack.

Hide in the shadows. Wait until everyone has gone. Then move quietly, using the ancient art of ninjutsu before, with a final look, pouncing on your prey—in this case, a toilet.

It's a typical part of the day for those who descend on the Japanese town of Iga (once home to a respected ninja of old) for the five-week-long Ninja Festival every April. People dressed as the deadly warriors perform dances and host impressive martial arts competitions, and spend time practicing their shuriken-throwing skills— these are the airborne star-shaped spiked objects that were part of the ninjas' infamous weaponry.

Many of the 30,000 visitors come dressed for the part as well, wearing the full gear of the stealth warrior, including his 'n' hers matching swords (plus small ones for the kids, too). People can be seen walking the streets of Iga clutching maps as they hunt out hidden life-sized mannequins of ninjas that are placed around the city as part of the festival. And those wanting to know more about the secret ways of the ninja can visit the Iga-ryu Ninja Museum, which boasts a ninja residence complete with revolving walls, trapdoors, and secret passageways. Disney World just doesn't cut it these days...

お手洗い
TOILET

MYSTERY OF THE NINJA The history of the ninja is one wrapped in myth and legend. What is known is that ninjas were a mercenary bunch who would carry out all manner of murder, espionage, sabotage, and theft for the right price. Their incredible talent for using stealth, disguises, and deadly weaponry made them feared throughout Japan. Images of ninjas in their iconic all-black clothes are believed to be inaccurate because black clothing would stand out too much in moonlight; it is more likely that they wore dark blue.

"The contest takes place under the statue of a famous kabuki actor who played the part of the hero Kagemasa. Kagemasa was a famously strong child, and Crying Sumo is held to pray for children's healthy growth."

Mainichi Daily News, *reporting on the Crying Sumo competition.*

You Big, Big Crybaby!

Hearing a baby screaming its head off is about as pleasant as having a tooth removed without anesthetic—just ask your parents. But at the Crying Sumo competition in Tokyo, Japan, hollering is positively encouraged. Every year, babies that are born in the area are brought to the Senso-ji temple to compete in a crying contest.

Each baby is held by a student sumo wrestler and then coaxed into crying by the wrestlers and the temple priest, who can wave their arms around and raise the baby above their heads to encourage the wee ones to start howling. If this fails, the sumo wrestlers can resort to putting on their scary fighting masks, which always seem to do the trick. Whichever baby cries first is declared the winner. If both babies should start bawling at exactly the same time, then the baby with the loudest cry is judged to be the winner. It may sound bizarre (and perhaps a little cruel), but the Japanese strongly believe that crying is very healthy for a baby.

A baby's crying can be as loud as 110 decibels—that's about the same as a power saw!

The Elvis of English...

... is how Li Yang has been described by his Chinese counterparts because of his remarkable Crazy English courses. These are no normal classroom-based lessons with a crusty, old teacher "drilling" his pupils on advanced grammar; no, Li likes to get on stage and teach crowds of up to 50,000 people to speak English all at the same time. His technique is not exactly orthodox—instead of lecturing on grammar and punctuation, his method is to get the audience to shout out words while gesturing wildly to emphasize the pronunciation of each selected word. It might sound crazy, but it is claimed that Li's techniques have helped more than 20 million people across Asia learn English...

SAY IT LOUD The idea for Crazy English came to Li Yang when he discovered that saying English words out loud helped him learn the language better. Before becoming a teacher in China, Li used to go to the top of his office building every morning and shout out English words at the top of his voice to improve his language skills!

"Now, stand firm and tall. Make a face. Get excited and yell it out—'I must do it. I can do it. I will do it. I will succeed!'"

Li Yang, *instructing his thousands of students.*

Don't think you are safe as a spectator, because competitors have been known to veer off into the assembled masses. And so has the runaway cheese!

"My God! It's not a hill; it's a cliff. People throw themselves down a cliff, after some cheese."
First-time cheese roller Chris Hodgkins.

Crazy for Cheese

The location of possibly the world's wackiest cheese event is Cooper's Hill in Gloucestershire, England. Every year, crowds amass to watch folk from all over the world take part in the infamous cheese-rolling event.

The premise is simple—there are five races. For each round, up to 20 people get ready at the top of the notoriously steep hill before the cheese is "released" and begins rolling down the hill. The competitors then have to chase it down the 604-foot/183-m near-vertical slope, and whoever reaches the bottom first is declared the

winner and gets to keep the beloved cheese. It's extremely difficult to run down the hill, so either sliding on your bottom (the coward's choice) or falling down head over heels is the usual way of descending in double time...

CHEESE WHEEL The type of cheese used in the event is the delicious 7-pound/3.2-kg Double Gloucester. This circular cheese reaches speeds up to 70 mph/112 kmh and takes just 12 seconds to reach the bottom.

One-Dollar Origami

Won Park has created a frog folded from a one-dollar bill that will actually jump once you release your finger from its back.

If you're ever searching for some unusual ideas of what to do with your money, then take inspiration from the amazing Won Park, the origami expert who has created all manner of folded paper objects from the humble U.S. dollar. From re-creating scenes from *Star Wars* and *Star Trek* to a toilet with its own lid, Hawaiian Won can create just about anything. The 38-year-old store co-owner has become a master of the ancient art after an incredible 32 years of practice.

ON THE MONEY
Even though his creations are mind-bogglingly intricate, Won insists that he never uses glue, tape, or cuts of any kind.

"There are some models that can take me three to four hours to complete. Then there are models that only take me 20 minutes. I guess the average time is about one and a half hours," explains Won Park.

Pont's epic collection of planes, bikes, and cars are available for the public to view at the museum at his chateau.

Jet fighters for Thrills, Not Kills

Although it is an extremely lucrative job, winemaking probably isn't the most exciting of all careers. So perhaps it isn't surprising that Frenchman Michel Pont collects planes in his spare time—namely jet fighters. Since 1985, he has owned up to 110 of them, which made him officially the biggest private collector of jet fighters in the world. The planes are kept on the site of his 16-hectare/40-acre vineyard of Château de Savigny-lès-Beaune in the Burgundy region of France. If he gets bored with looking over his aircraft collection, he can always take to the road on one of his 300 motorbikes or in one of his 34 Abarth Fiat racing cars. Mon Dieu!

Michel is unable to take off in any of the planes from his huge vineyard because the fighters are banned from use in French airspace.

Pole Position

Becoming a winner at the annual Independence Day celebrations in Indonesia is a slippery affair. Trying to climb your way up an oil-coated tree trunk in the *panjat pinang* competition is hard enough, but then you have to worry about fellow competitors pulling you down during your ascent as they try to get past you. Trousers, in particular, are at risk of being torn off.

So why bother? Well, it's because of the prizes that can be found at the top of the poles—these can range from the humdrum, such as plastic buckets and towels, to bicycles and keys for a brand-new motorbike. We reckon the prizes are probably worth having your bottom exposed for the whole world to see!

Many believe that the climb up the greasy pole to reap the prizes at the top is the perfect representation of Indonesia's past struggle for independence. The country was released from Dutch colonial rule in 1945 and has not looked back (or down) since.

STAR ENTRY

Most Preposterous Pastime

It's the best food fight in the world and everyone is invited...

To start the world's biggest food fight in Buñol, Spain, someone from the vast crowd of people gathered in the town's square must scramble up to the top of a greasy pole and grab the leg of ham that's been placed on top. Then, water cannons spray the crowds, T-shirts are thrown, and trucks arrive carrying 140 tons of tomatoes amassed from the surrounding countryside. More than 40,000 people then arm themselves and start pummeling each other with the fruity missiles over the following two hours. That's the premise for the now world-famous La Tomatina event held every year in the town. What's not to like about it?

A BRIEF HISTORY OF TOMATO FIGHTING
Organizers claim that the tomato war started in August 1945. In the village square of Buñol, a fight broke out between youths during a festival, which grew to a full-blown food fight as they grabbed tomatoes from a market stall. The fight was so much fun that they did it again the following year.

During its early years, tomato fighting was banned. But in 1955, the people of Buñol decided that they wanted the event to be made official and voiced their protest to the ban. They marched through the streets to the music of a funeral march while carrying a coffin containing a large tomato. The authorities relented and La Tomatina was here to stay.

RULES OF ENGAGEMENT
Before the public are allowed to unleash a torrent of tomatoes on everyone around them, there are rules that must be obeyed:

1. All tomatoes must be crushed before being thrown.
2. Glass bottles and other items, which could be extremely dangerous in such a setting, are banned.
3. Tearing clothes is forbidden.
4. Wearing flip-flops is officially a very stupid idea.
5. The best advice is to wear goggles (preferably diver's masks for maximum face coverage) to protect your eyes from a bruising encounter...

"Never, and we mean never, climb on a gate, window, wall, etc. to be able to watch the battle; you will become the target of 40,000 people."
The golden rule given on the event's official web site.

Tall Stories

> Children are used to finish off the top of the towers because they are so light and agile.

The famous biannual Castells Competition held in the Catalonian city of Tarragona in the south of Spain sees *colles* (the groups that make up the towers) gather together in the city's bullfighting ring to outdo their competitors at building the highest and most complex human tower.

The technique is complicated as the base of the castell is created by heavyset *castellers*, who are surrounded and supported by a mass of people to act as the foundations for the human tower—these foundations are known as the *pinya* (pineapple). Then there is a rush as the rest of the castellers leap into action, forming the tower as quickly but as carefully as possible.

> The towers can reach up to 49 feet/15 m in height.

Once completed, the final casteller who reaches the top must hold one hand up high and point four fingers outward—this represents the stripes on the Catalan flag. Of course, what goes up must come down, and watching the castellers remove themselves from the tower is like witnessing a life-sized version of Jenga, the game where players must remove one of the wooden blocks making up a tower in the hope that their piece doesn't cause the whole group to collapse...

Feathered Friends

> The world record for the biggest collection of owl memorabilia is officially listed under the name Dianne Turner—she was the lady who collected all of the items in the first place before Pam bought them after her death. In tribute to Dianne, Pam let Turner keep her name as the record holder.

Replying to an advertisement can net you a world record, as American Pam Barker found out when she offered to buy a hoard of owl collectibles from a weekly classified-ads magazine. When she first saw the ad, it stated that there were 14,000 pieces of owl memorabilia up for sale, but Pam thought that it must be a mistake and be a more realistic 1,400. It turned out to be correct, and she ended up buying 18,055 items for a reduced price. Pam figured that the huge collection must be a world record, and after making some inquiries, she was proved right.

> **"My husband would like his store back."**
> *Pam Barker on how her collection lives in her partner's building supply store.*

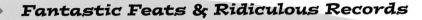

Wash Away Your Woes

If you should find yourself in Thailand between the dates of April 13 and 15, it's best to make sure your fancy camera is tucked away safely. Why? Well, because once a year Thai people like to take to the streets armed with water pistols, buckets of water, waterlogged sponges, and the odd elephant or three to douse residents and tourists alike with glorious H_2O in celebration of Songkran, the official start of the Buddhist New Year.

The festival represents the time for cleansing oneself, fresh for the start of the Buddhist New Year.

If the idea of street-to-street water fighting is appealing, then the northern city of Chiang Mai is the best place to go. Surrounded by a square moat (which offers an ideal source of water for refilling your weaponry), there is no escaping being doused as thousands of Thai folk and tourists mix it up.

POLICE HELP ME! Don't think the police will come running to help if you want some time out from the watery fun; they're also happy to be sprayed and will most likely be doused by the gangs riding around in pickup trucks, ready to dump water on any officer unfortunate enough to be standing directing traffic. You have been warned!

Wife Wars

Sometimes, love can become a drag. Quite literally. Created in Sonkajärvi, Finland, the Wife Carrying Championships may have started out as a bit of a joke back in 1992, but since then, the wife-carrying craze has swept the planet with the U.S., China, Britain, Italy, and Australia all slinging wives over their backs before taking on an 830-foot/253-m assault course. The track features two obstacles that competitors need to heave themselves over and also a water obstacle to be waded through. Among other things, the champion receives the equivalent of his wife's weight in beer. Now it all makes sense!

Yes, There Are Rules!

You may think it all sounds a bit silly but there are strict rules:

- If any man drops his wife, he will be fined 15 seconds.
- The wife being carried doesn't have to be married to the competitor.
- All wives must be over 17 years old.
- All the participants "must have fun" (even as they fall flat on their faces...).

"The wives and the wife carriers are not afraid of challenges or burdens. They push their way persistently forward, holding tightly, generally with a twinkle in the eyes."

From the Wife Carrying Championships official web site.

The Vikings Are Back!

The Vikings were a tough bunch who struck terror into the hearts of any nation who happened to be raided by them. Not the Scots, though—after all, they're not known for being timid, so it seems only fitting that the Scottish island of Shetland should celebrate the arrival of the Vikings more than 1,000 years ago, considering they themselves were ruled by the horned ones for 600 years.

This festival is just one of nine similar events that occur on the island every year, but this one is the most impressive and also boasts of being the biggest fire festival in Europe.

The Up Helly Aa Festival is held every year in January, and you can witness the astonishing main event, which sees a squad of men (dressed up as scary-as-heck-looking Vikings) marching through the streets of the Lerwick, dragging a 29-foot/9-m replica of a Viking galley along with them. If that wasn't impressive enough, they're followed by more than 900 "guisers"—folk dressed in various disguises. Once the procession reaches its end, the boat is set on fire amid music and fireworks. After the boat has been reduced to a cinder, a traditional Viking evening of beer and indecency follows!

Air Guitar Hero

It's official—music lessons are boring. But there is hope for those who want to experience the awe of being a guitar hero—the Air Guitar World Championships, held in Finland each year. Competitors must show off their air guitar skills to two 60-second songs—one selected by the organizers and one of the competitor's own choosing. Using only body movement and ludicrous facial expressions to create that amazing guitar performance, no real instruments are allowed (although you can use a plectrum if you so desire), but you can air guitar either on an electric or acoustic guitar (or both). Personal air roadies are welcome.

Top Tracks

Here is a selection of songs that have been dished out by the organizers for the air guitarists to rock to over the years:

2007 **Ozzy Osbourne: "I Don't Wanna Stop"**

2005 **Green Day: "American Idiot"**

2003 **The Darkness: "Get Your Hands Off of My Woman"**

2000 **Motörhead: "Ace of Spades"**

1999 **Guns 'n' Roses: "Locomotive"**

1998 **Lenny Kravitz: "Are You Gonna Go My Way"**

1997 **Nirvana: "Smells Like Teen Spirit"**

"It's impossible to be angry and play air guitar." Zac Monro, Air Guitar World Champion 2001 and 2002.

Silly Sports

You have to be the fittest of the fittest, the best of the best, to make it as a superstar athlete...

For some sports, you need to be more than just brilliant—you need to be as mad as a hatter as well. After all, if you're going to perform martial arts underwater (see page 66), you need to be in tip-top shape—but having a screw loose obviously helps you get in the water in the first place.

And even those who may not have the most muscular of physiques needn't worry—being crazy could see you winning gold anyway. Well, a trophy in the shape of a crushed beer can, that is, if you're talented enough to win the Dumpster Dive in the Redneck Games in Georgia (see page 72). Even frustrated motor-racing wannabes can make their mark by buying themselves a secondhand lawn mower and taking part in a 12-hour race to claim victory (see page 69).

So no matter what shape or size, you too can become a world-class, competition-slaying super sports hero because there is a silly sport out there for just about everybody.

Boxing Clever

Although cynics may guffaw at the outlandishly brilliant World Chess Boxing Championships, we think that the event simply shows how "versatile" boxers can be. Chess boxing sees two extremely intelligent fighters alternating between punching each other and then sitting down in the middle of the ring for a game of chess. There are a total of 11 rounds (unless there is a knockout or the dreaded checkmate): six rounds of chess in four-minute rounds and five rounds of fisticuffs that last three minutes each.

If no one is knocked out or has declared "checkmate" after 11 rounds, then the fight is decided on the points earned during the boxing bouts. If that is also a tie, then whoever had control of the black pieces on the board wins. Hardly fair!

Boxers Frank Stoldt from Germany and David Depto from the USA slug it out in the picture, right, in the first Chess Boxing Light Heavyweight Championship in Berlin, in 2007. Stoldt won, pawns down.

The World Chess Boxing Organization's (yes, there really is one) official slogan is "Fighting is done in the ring and wars are waged on the board."

"One minute you're having your skull battered, the next you're sat down trying to work out why you appear to have 48 pawns, let alone what to do with them," writes ringside reporter Georgina Turner.

On a Wing and a Prayer...

...And you really had better pray that you're not blown off the wing of a parked Airbus A340 by wind and rain if you enter the Swing On The Wing contest held in Abu Dhabi, in United Arab Emirates. The competition sees pro and amateur golf players stand on a plane's wing and try to hit the ball as far as they can. The winner in 2007 was European Tour star Henrik Stenson, who smashed the ball 721 yards/659 m. Now, that's what we call a first-class performance.

The world record holder of the longest drive (golf hit) is the U.K.'s Paul Slater, who smashed his own previous record in 2006 by driving a shot for 884 yards/808 m the following year. The long-driving competition is held at an airfield in Britain every year.

Spectators could watch from behind a large glass wall that offered a perfect view of all the bizarre events.

On Your Marks, Get Set...Glug!

Hearing the firing pistol underwater must have been one of the easier things to do if you were competing in the Underwater Olympics. In 2008, Qiandao Underwater World in China decided to beat Beijing at its own games by holding a special underwater sporting event. Dressed in wet suits and laden with scuba gear, divers undertook a host of events, including fencing, ring tossing, gymnastics, hurdles, and shooting.

Trying to keep your balance while fighting the weight of the water made the games punishing for the divers. For example, to make life even more difficult for the divers who were taking part in the shooting event, they had to stand on a metal wire before trying to hit the target—an inflated balloon placed 16 feet/5 m away from them. After all, the whole point of any Olympic event is that it has to push the athletes to their limits—and we think they succeeded admirably with the Underwater Olympics.

The Korean sign in the background of the martial arts event translates as "Let's cheer together! Water Olympics."

Team Spirit

Other countries also got involved with the underwater mentalism with the Coex Aquarium in Seoul, Korea, holding its own event. Their roster of sports included underwater soccer, weightlifting, tae kwon do and, um, grass hockey. Amazingly, play wasn't called off because of a waterlogged pitch...

For the 2008 competition, there were 299 runners, 42 horses, and 74 relay teams competing in the marathon.

Galloping to Victory

There must be something in the water in Wales, because not only is the town of Llanwrtyf Wells famous for its bog-snorkeling event (see page 54), but the town's residents have also dreamed up a way of making marathons more interesting. After all, why have mere humans racing against each other when you can have humans versus horses over a 22-mile/35-km course across the moorlands? It shouldn't come as a huge surprise to learn that the horses have cantered off with the top prize every time. That is, until the 25th anniversary of the event, in 2004, which saw competitor Huw Lobb beat the fastest horse by an incredible two minutes. Since the creation of the event all those years ago, £1,000 had been put aside each year for the person who did eventually win. So 25 years later, Huw ended up with a check for an incredible £25,000 (approximately $50,000)!

There was more horse humiliation when in 2007, two runners beat the fastest horse. The horse camp blamed the overly hot weather for the defeat. What a nightmare.

A BOLD CLAIM The ridiculous marathon came about when a regular at the Neuadd Arms pub in the town claimed that a human could beat a horse across country if the distance was long enough. The landlord of the pub decided that it was a theory worth investigating and the mad marathon was born.

Big Bungee

There are individuals who like to bungee-jump into volcanoes and couples who enjoy jumping together in the nude, but seeing this group of 25 crazy men and women make a jump together has to be the most absurd. The mass jump (unofficially the world's biggest) was performed in 1998 from a platform that was suspended in front of the twin towers of the Deutsche Bank headquarters in Germany. The jump saw the tightly-packed-together group plummeting 170 feet/52 m before bouncing back up. Here's hoping nobody had their lunch beforehand...

The previous record for the most people to bungee-jump stood at a mere 12 and was set in 1994 in Helsinki, Finland.

Wacky Racers

We're used to fast cars going at ridiculous speeds around racetracks, but if you want real silliness, then look no further than these madcap racing sports!

Vroom, Vroom Eeyore...

They may not look like the world's most pure racing thoroughbreds, but donkey racing is massively popular the world over, from kids racing them at Dunton Stables in the West Midlands, Britain (no whips or spurs allowed) and the donkey derbies featured in festivals all over the world (including Santas racing theirs in the Swiss Alps) to professional jockey Pavel Bradik, pictured here on donkey Else during a donkey-riding race in Hanover, Germany.

> Some riders sit backward—they believe it makes it easier to pat the donkey, so it goes faster.

> The most ever paid for a racing donkey was $50,000 or £25,000.

> The event also has a beauty contest to find the best-looking buffalo.

Get a Mooove On!

Forget the elegant sport of horse racing, which sees people in silly hats watching short people racing around a beautifully tended racetrack on horseback. No, we're more interested in the rough and (literally) tumble of the annual water buffalo festival in Chonburi, Thailand. At the heart of the festivities is buffalo racing down a "drag" strip roughly 330 feet/100 m long.

Riders race along the course with no saddle or stirrups, clinging on to the buffalo's loose skin for dear life as the animals either rush down to the finish line or decide to do their own thing and not bother finishing—or worse still, think the best way of dealing with such a race is to do everything possible to throw the jockey off their back.

> Some say that the racing was started as a way of celebrating the forthcoming rice harvest, whereas others believe that the tradition began hundreds of years ago when two farmers got into an argument over whose buffalo was the fastest...

MOO POWER NEEDED! In the old days, all buffalo would be used to work in the fields to help with the rice harvest and locals believed that racing them helped the buffalo work faster. Nowadays, the farmers are increasingly turning to the pulling power of tractors, so more and more buffalo are being reared purely for the honor of racing.

To celebrate the association's 25th anniversary in 1997, competitors raced nonstop for 25 hours instead of the usual 12!

Mowing Down the Competition

Who doesn't dream of being a world-record-beating driver? Whether it's NASCAR, Formula 1 racing, or kicking up dirt while rallying in the World Rally Championships, the dream of crossing the line is thwarted by one problem—you need to be very rich as well as talented. Instead, you can try British lawn mower racing, the perfect cheap and cheerful way to become a "racing driver." The British Lawn Mower Racing Association is the king of mow-town racing and boasts four different classes for potential racers—from Class One, which is hand-pushed mowers, to Class Four, which features wheel-based mowers that can achieve speeds of up to 50 mph/80 kmh.

The BLMRA's annual 12-hour race sees up to three people per mower racing through the night to see who can cover the 300-mile/482-km track the fastest!

Fans past and present have included the actor Oliver Reed and British racing legend Stirling Moss.

A riderless ostrich can run as fast as a racehorse, with a top speed of 40 mph/64 kmh.

Feathered Speed Fiends

They may look like they should be in the "Absurd Animals" chapter, but ostriches are not always the object of ridicule—they can cover ground as quickly as a racehorse and are seriously dangerous and aggressive too.

Those adventurous enough to attempt ostrich racing may be brave, but they do look utterly ridiculous in the process. For some, like the ostrich farmer workers based at the Highgate Ostrich Farm in Oudtshoorn, South Africa, racing is a daily event as they take to the track to show spectators just how fast the ostriches can move. Spectators are kept a safe distance away...

"An ostrich that hasn't been worked with can be very cantankerous. They can kill you. And if they catch you out in the open, you can't outrun them." Joe Hedrick, ostrich expert, explains the perils of working with the birds.

OBEY THE RULES! You can imagine just how heated the world's largest and oldest soccer game can get, so the organizers have made it clear that no one must intentionally harm anyone. Anxious types should be reassured further by ancient rules that state that nobody may murder anyone during the course of the match either. Phew!

Shrove Soccer

The Brits are bonkers about soccer—they like to get dressed up in their team colors, watch the match, drink too much, throw up, and then start hitting each other. It's a strange pastime, but nothing compared with the brilliantly silly but oh-so-slightly scary Shrovetide soccer match held once a year in Ashbourne, Britain. Known as "no rules" soccer, the premise is simple: Two teams made up of opposing folk from opposite ends of the town play a game of soccer where the respective team goals are 3 miles/ 4.8 km apart. The match boasts hundreds of players and is played over two days, with each half of the match lasting a staggering eight hours!

The wacky soccer match is believed to be up to 1,000 years old, and some reckon that in olden times, a severed head fresh from an execution was used to play the game instead of a soccer ball...

To score a goal, you need to tap the ball three times against a specially built stone goal plinth.

Cowadunga!

The Swiss are not known for their frivolity, but judging from the Cow Dung Golf Tournament, they're learning to let their hair down at last. Now in its third successful year, this smelly sport sees competitors marching up the Swiss Alps where cattle roam free, before seeing who can hit the most piles of cow poo within a two-hour period. Normal golf clubs are used (and abused) during this 120-minute poo-fest, and one can only imagine the mess you and your golf gear are left in once the dung has settled.

Stuck Between a Rock and...Paper and Scissors

Although you might think of rock, paper, scissors as something that you only ever played at school, it is actually now a full-blown professional sport. Not convinced? Well, how does winning a check for $50,000 sound to you? It's the prize money that was won at the Bud Light/USA Rock Paper Scissors League Tournament that was televised in 2008. The winner, Sean Sears, also won a trip to compete against international champions at the International Rock Paper Scissors Federation Championship, which was being held alongside the Olympics in Beijing, where he won the bronze.

More Weapons, Please!
Some players have been known to introduce "trump" moves such as dynamite. However, there is some dispute over whether dynamite would actually win—paper could beat a stick of dynamite because it would smother the wick! There's also a version that features 22 different objects, including guns, lightning, axes, fire, snakes, and nuclear weapons.

"Facing off against the finest rock, paper, scissors players in the world was an intense challenge that pushed my skills to the limit." Mark Cleland, winner of the International Rock Paper Scissors Federation Championship, held in Beijing.

The only boring aspect of the game is the view spectators are confronted with—a mass of limbs with the ball hidden from view under the heaving bodies of the players.

All-Out Wall!

It's the sport for swanky people only. First, you'll need to qualify to get into the famous Eton College in Britain and then you'll need parents with the world's deepest pockets to pay the fees. Once there, you can mix it up with the world's finest folk—past pupils have included Princes William and Harry (both pictured, Harry center, William leaning, right)—and indulge in the ancient sport known as the Eton Wall Game. This sees players, who are split into two teams, head to a wall at the school and then battle it out to try to get the ball from one end of the wall to the other using their feet. The outcome is usually goalless as students simply pile up against the wall and dive into anyone unfortunate enough to have the ball in their possession. Not very gentlemanly.

If you ever find yourself with your face pushed up against the wall during a match, at least try to go for a "shy"—this is where the ball is pushed up against the wall, off the ground, by a person's feet before being touched by the player's hand. For this straining effort, the team is awarded a point.

No "sneaking" or "knuckling" are allowed. Apparently.

STAR ENTRY

"All profit—every last cent—from the Redneck Games goes to local charities. We don't make a dime. Never have. Never will. That's not what it's about." Mac Davis, creator of the Redneck Games.

Most Silly Sport

Yes sirrree, welcome to the Redneck Games, the true sport of the US of A...

Home of pickup trucks, hunting rifles, and beer guzzling, East Dublin, Georgia, loves to celebrate that most revered (or reviled) of traditions: being a redneck. Started in 1996 as a small event to entertain the locals and to gently mock the Olympic Games being held in Atlanta up the road, the Redneck Games have become a national institution attracting thousands of people every summer.

The events are what every self-respecting redneck should love—see the box, right, for more details—but if the idea of throwing yourself into a trash bin to find prizes or showing off your butt crack to crowds of thousands of people sounds like fun, then you now know where to go. Good luck!

> The prize for most of the events is a trophy with a crushed beer can at the top of it.

> The word *redneck* began life as a description of people who work in the outdoors and whose necks become sunburned from toiling outside all day long.

GOING FOR GOLD
Here are some of the redneck games you can expect to see and what you'll need to do to win:

Toilet Seat Horseshoes
Take one lightweight plastic toilet seat (while crossing your fingers that it's clean) and throw it carefully, aiming for a stake in the ground. Did we say a stake? We meant toilet plunger, of course. The person who lands the seat over the handle of the plunger is the winner.

Armpit Serenade
Create the loudest, boldest, and best trump by cupping your hand under your armpit and flapping your elbow up and down like a mad chicken to squeeze out the trapped air. If you can play a well-known tune, then you're guaranteed to be a big hit with the crowds.

Mud-Pit Belly Flop
"The fatter, the better" is the best rule to follow for any contestant wanting to make a huge splash by leaping flabby belly first into a pool of mud. Winners are judged on style and how big a splash they manage to make.

Other Highlights
Hubcap Hurl—see how far you can throw a hubcap!
Butt Crack Competition—do you have the best butt crack poking out of the top of your jeans?
Seed-Spittin' Contest—how far can you spit a seed?

Iron(ing) Man

Well, if you're going to iron your pants, then why not do it up the side of a mountain? Enter extreme ironing, a sport that sees its ironing evangelists showing the world just how daring pressing your boxer shorts can be when you're hanging off the side of a cliff.

The first and apparently only championships for daredevils with a passion for pristinely pressed pants was the Extreme Ironing World Championship held in Germany in 2002. Competitors had to grab their ruffled clothes, irons, and ironing boards and proceed to iron in a variety of bizarre locations. These included climbing a wall while pressing clothes, ironing while halfway up a tree, and ironing while hurtling down a river in a rubber ring. Ten countries competed, with Britain coming out on top.

Shaw came up with the idea for extreme ironing when confronted by a pile of laundry at home and decided that he needed to make ironing more interesting. He succeeded.

The sport of extreme ironing faces a very real threat from the Urban Housework group, who have introduced such extreme sports as mop-jousting, apocalypse dishwashing, downhill vacuuming, and inner-city clothes drying...

"Ironists are sometimes so absorbed in getting themselves into some sort of awkward or dangerous situation with their ironing board that they forget the main reason they are there in the first place: to rid their clothing of creases and wrinkles." Phil Shaw, creator of extreme ironing.

Rolling Down the Road

Perhaps the cheapest sport known to man, road bowling sees competitors hurling a 1.7-pound/ 0.8-kg iron bowl down a closed-off public road and whoever completes the 2.5-mile/4-km course with the fewest throws is declared the winner. It is very popular in Ireland, where large crowds can gather around the throwers, so if you're an overly enthusiastic spectator who enjoys getting close to the action, don't be surprised if you end up getting a ball of iron in your face!

In the past, the winner was decided by who could get the ball the farthest in 20 throws.

Is It a Bird? Is It a Plane?

No, it's a Bognor Birdman, actually, one of many men and women who attend the seaside town of Bognor Regis in England each year to throw themselves off the pier in the hope of winning the prize for traveling the farthest distance. This is achieved using bizarre flying contraptions that competitors build. Many are just plain ridiculous and designed to simply make the spectators laugh as competitors plunge into the sea from a great height. After all, just how far do you think you would get flying in a toilet or a giant hedgehog?

There is a serious side, though, as a few committed engineers build gliders to try to beat the current distance—292 ft/89 m— set by Dave Bradshaw back in 1992. If anyone manages to fly 328 feet/100 m, they will be awarded £25,000 for their troubles.

The 2008 Bognor Birdman event was actually held in Worthing because the end of Bognor's pier has been demolished!

Some of the crazy characters people have dressed as include the pope, Donald Duck, Doctor Who (complete with Tardis), four ninja turtles, Wonder Woman, and a chicken-and-mushroom pie.

Crazy Golf, Meet Wacky Baseball...

... Well, sort of. It's actually extremely difficult to describe the silly Swiss sport of Hornussen, other than it looks utterly ridiculous. So let's start with the basics. The player thwacks a small, rubber puck called a Hornuss mounted on a launcher with his bizarre fishing-rod-style 6.5-foot/2-m bendy club. The hornuss then whizzes through the air at up to 199 mph/320 kmh—but there are no holes for it to land in. Instead, it shoots toward the opposing team of up to 18 players, who are all lined up in a field and holding Schindels; these are wooden placards that are used to try to catch the hornuss as it hurtles toward them.

If the team manages to catch the puck, the striker gets no points; however, if the puck gets through, then points are awarded depending on how far the ball managed to get on landing. You see? It is crazy, and we suspect not very pleasant for any player unfortunate enough to be hit by the Hornuss!

There are more than 200 clubs and 8,500 players dedicated to the sport of Hornussen in Switzerland.

The puck is called a Hornuss because of the noise it makes when going through the air—in English, the word translates as "hornet."

> Prizes are suitably simple but sophisticated— bronze, silver, and gold cravats.

I Say, How Marvelous!

Spiffing, eh what, chaps? If you're sick and tired of oafish behavior and just plain bad manners, then one would recommend putting on one's finest suit (from London's Savile Row, of course) and partaking in the sport of gentlemen known as the Chap Olympics. Yes, it's a hark back to a finer day when one would open doors for ladies and know how to conduct oneself in public.

Now, let's translate the above—the founders of these mad Olympics are Gustav Temple and Torquil Arbuthnot, who decided back in the early 21st century that they'd had enough of people behaving badly, acting like lager louts, and walking around in sportswear all the time. Their solution? To set up a magazine called *The Chap* and, more important, to create an event that would act as a shining beacon to proper behavior while keeping its tongue firmly in its well-groomed cheek. So once a year, folk turn up in their finest suits and dresses, and indulge in such ridiculous sports as The Three-Trousered Limbo, The Pipe Smoker's Relay, and Cucumber Sandwich Discus.

PROVE YOUR GENTLEMANLINESS!
The events at the Chap Olympics strive to bring out the best in gentlemanly conduct, including the following:

Bounders
Six chaps are given two minutes to behave appallingly to six ladies. Once suitably offended, the ladies must slap the chaps and whichever cad is on the receiving end of the loudest slap is declared the winner! Tally-ho!

Shouting at Foreigners
Not as beastly as it sounds, as the chaps must deal with a non-English-speaking shopkeeper and try to buy everything a proper gentleman needs to cope in life, such as a trouser press and kippers.

Lobster Moustache Dueling
As pictured here (left), the competing chaps must attack each other's beards and moustaches with lobsters! I say!

TOKEN GESTURE Even finding the event requires gentlemanly cunning and intellectual prowess. Well, sort of. Working from clues, one must collect tokens from properly posh shops to find out the exact location of the Olympics. For example, in 2008, one was required to enter the shop JJ Fox & Robert and say, "I need a pipe tobacco that will last a hundred-yard sprint" before a token was handed over.

"If you must engage in sporting activity, and I can't really see why that would be necessary, old-fashioned white canvas plimsolls are perfectly adequate. Or brogues with a strong sole."

Gustav Temple explains to a news reporter when asked about wearing sneakers for sport. Such attire is strictly forbidden at the Chap Olympics.

The Crazy Crew

Why be a nut all by yourself when it's far more fun having crazy company?

They say that people have strength in numbers. Well, judging from the following chapter, it simply gives people more of an excuse to behave as if they are stark raving mad. Nothing wrong with that, of course, because it means that the rest of us can look on and watch groups of people doing the craziest things. Many would claim they are doing it for a good reason, such as for charity, but we reckon it's because they have one or possibly a few screws loose!

After all, why would you want to dress up as a storm trooper and march down a California street (see page 77)? Or risk slamming into your friends at 100 mph/161 kmh in nothing but a glorified batsuit (see page 82)? Or for that matter, dress up as an Italian plumber usually found leaping over mushrooms in a video game (see page 83)?

Perhaps we should take a page out of their book (and this one!) and go a little crazy with friends once in a while to let off some steam.

STAR ENTRY

The Maddest Bunch

No other film series has induced more fan worship than the legendary Star Wars. Here, we profile the best of the best of the crazy fans!

Going Down a Storm

The 501st Legion is planet Earth's biggest group of organized *Star Wars* fans who love to dress up in homemade storm trooper costumes. The force is strong in this lot, because they have more than 3,300 members from more than 30 countries.

In early 2007, 200 501st Legion members marched down the streets of Pasadena, California, raising money for charity. George Lucas, the film series creator, was on hand as well to offer praise for the dedication of the 501st State.

"For the past eight years, I had been wearing my armor with only a few other members in China, but here I am surrounded by so many of my fellow troopers and it feels like a real family." Roy Waung, member of the 501st Legion's Taiwan Garrison.

Jedi Gym Class

Ever hoped for a workout with a difference? Well, the Ludosport Lightsaber Combat Academy in Milan, Italy, offers just that. People are flocking to the Jedi academy to learn seven different styles of Jedi combat. As well as brushing up on how to brandish a light saber without taking your eye out, you can also learn how to stop Darth Maul with a throw and whip Darth Vader's light saber out of his clutches!

To get students in shape for defending themselves from the blaster rounds fired by the 501st Legion (above), instructors throw balls at students that they deflect with their light sabers.

Laugh Off Your Troubles

Feeling sad, lonely, or depressed? Then snap out of it and grow a spine! Sorry, we mean, why not take after the people pictured here, who are attending World Laughter Day, an event designed to giggle away your blues? It's no laughing matter either (well, it is but...), because tickling your funny bone on purpose can bring down stress and anxiety levels and even strengthen your immune system. Apparently.

At the heart of all this hilarity is the "Guru of Giggling" Dr. Madan Kataria, who created Laughter Yoga in 1995. It proved so successful that he has now taught people the principles of laughter therapy in more than 60 countries—and there are now more than 6,000 laughter clubs all over the planet.

> Toddlers can laugh up to 400 times a day, whereas adults can manage only 7 to 15 times a day.

> Policemen in Allahabad, India, regularly use laughter therapy at the beginning of their grueling working day to lift their spirits. On the other side of the cell bars, some prisoners in the U.S., Europe, and India are also known to be practicing the therapy.

HOW TO LAUGH... No, you're not going to need a bumper-sized book of jokes to get you and your friends ready for a spot of laughter therapy—there is actually a technique you can learn to induce laughter without the need for bad punch lines. In a group of people, you all start by faking the laughter and over time (and with practice), you will find that it becomes genuine because it is so infectious.

When It's OK to Drink the Bathwater...

If your parents have been moaning about being overworked and stressed, perhaps you should recommend the Yunessun Spa Resort in Hakone, Japan, as the ideal way to stop whining and start winning, well, wining, instead. In 2007, guests at the resort enjoyed the delights of bathing in a spa that was filled with Beaujolais Nouveau wine. Staff were also on hand to pour glasses of wine to those who simply couldn't get enough booze and were tempted to drink directly from the pool (that also contained bathwater additives)—something that was a no-no, according to the spa's rules.

Actually, we think you would have been crazy to drink from the pool itself—although the grapes that make wine are traditionally crushed by feet, you don't want to be drinking the wine while the feet are still in it. Anyone for a red wine with hint of oak and athlete's foot?

BATH BY BEER Does bathing in wine sound disgusting to you? Well, surely it can't be as bad as another spa in Hakone that offered its patrons the chance to submerge themselves in a whirlpool tub filled with water colored to the shade of beer and smelling of barley and hops. Those who love their boozy bathwater were glad to hang around, though, because staff popped in and out three times a day, dousing the bathers with fresh beer. Yep, we know what you're thinking: gross.

What is believed to be the world's longest barbecue was pulled off by a group of Russians in 2008 who built a barbie that stretched 334 feet/102 m long. To fill it up with food for grilling, it took 500 sausages and 250 meaty skewers!

"Slap 61,729 lbs/ 28,000 kg of Beef on the Barbie!"

The people of Paraguay must have eyes bigger than their bellies because they're the current record holders of the world's largest one-day open-air barbecue. More than 30,000 people helped set the world record and wolfed down an astonishing 61,729 pounds/ 28,000 kg of beef in six hours. The food was cooked in an area 328 feet/100 m long by 197 feet/60 m wide where chefs lit fires to cook the mountain of meat. Alas, not everyone was happy; some people complained that there wasn't enough food to eat! It seems you can't please all of the people all of the time...

The name of the event was *Todo bicho que camina va al asador*, which translates into "Every critter walking goes to the barbecue."

"All of the food that was there was eaten. It's the largest quantity of meat that has been eaten at one event held on one day."
Ralph Hannah, judge at the world's biggest barbecue.

Weird Science

Right, here's a "scientific" experiment for you (and one to be carried out only with supervision from your parents and in an outside area). Take a large bottle of Diet Coke and then drop a pack of Mentos candies into it. Be sure that your face is not hovering over the top of the bottle or else you could find yourself with a mint-induced black eye. Why? Well, because of the reaction the candies have with the Coke, the sugary liquid will shoot out of the top of the bottle and can reach dizzying heights of up to 33 feet/10 m!

These sickly fountains have become all the rage, and students in Riga, Latvia, set off an amazing 1,911 such geysers at the same time to create a new world record. Looks like they had fun!

The previous world record stood at 1,360 fountains.

DANGER! There is a rumor going around that if you should eat a Mentos right after drinking some Diet Coke, the reaction in your stomach could prove fatal. Although there have been no reported deaths caused by a lethal Mentos/Diet Coke mix, do you really want to find out if it's an urban myth or not? We recommend you don't try this at home. Seriously.

Coke Conundrum

There are many theories as to why the candies react so violently with the Coke. Some believe that it's because of the acidic nature of Coke, but others reckon it's because every Mentos candy has thousands of tiny pores. They soak up the carbon dioxide in the drink as the candy sinks to the bottom of the bottle, which then causes the fountain to erupt.

Swim Club

You might not associate China with being boiling hot, but in summer the temperatures can get so high and the air so smothering that the locals rush to the nearest swimming pool to cool off. Pictured here is a pool in Suining in the province of Sichuan on a day where temperatures topped a scorching 99°F/37°C. We're not too sure just how hygienic it was in there—after all, honestly ask yourself, Could you face plowing your way through that mass of people and inflated life rings to make it out of the pool to get to the toilet in time? Honestly? Yuck!

The Real City of Angels

Everyone in the city got involved—the youngest snow angel was six-week-old baby Jack Deitz and the oldest participant was 99-year-old Pauline Jaeger.

Los Angeles, the city of angels, has been replaced. That's right—by the city of Bismarck, North Dakota. The city managed to show off 8,962 "snow angels" when the city's residents turned up on the cold morning of December 26, 2007, and threw themselves onto their backs on the state capitol grounds before proceeding to wave their arms madly up and down. It all may look extremely silly, but the record-setting event was a matter of honor for the city. After all, they set the original record back in 2002—of 1,791 crazy people—but their rivals in Michigan stole their thunder in 2006 with 3,784 even crazier people. Well, they do say revenge is a dish best served cold. Or in this case, with a side order of icicles and frostbite...

Make Your Mark

Making the perfect snow angel requires, well...not much skill, but you need to nail the basics to make your mark properly. Ensure that you're properly dressed in winter clothes before getting a bunch of people standing in a line on some clean snow. Then lie down flat in the snow and start moving your arms and legs out and in—just like you would for a star jump. Then get someone to help you up while trying not to disturb your angelic masterpiece. Now all you need is 8,962 people to join you and you can set a new world record. Simple!

"It's fun and puts us on the map. People think there's nothing going on up here," says Edna Arvidson, Bismarck resident, to the Associated Press.

Strictly Scuba

Seventy-four scuba divers amassed at the bottom of a pool may sound like a large crowd in need of an open ocean, but there is a reason for this somewhat extreme gathering— they're all taking a dance class while trying to keep in sequence for longer than ten minutes. Well, these flipper-footed Australian scuba divers (left) managed to do just that and set a world record in the process. They held an underwater dance class at Sydney's Olympic Park Aquatic Centre and did an entire sequence that lasted for 13 minutes and 20 seconds. No explanation was given for how the dancers managed to hear the music at the bottom of the pool, though!

If the idea of scuba ballroom dancing doesn't float your boat or flap your flippers, then you can always have a go at underwater ballet, like Olympic medal–winning Miho Takeda did in Tokyo in July 2008.

Falling Down

It's bonkers, but there are people out there who enjoy hurtling toward the ground very, very quickly. Meet the world's wackiest skydivers!

The same core team intends to break the record again in 2009 with 99 skydivers.

"Our biggest concern is a collision in the sky. A collision in the sky would knock you out or break bones."
Justin Shorb, before the world-record-breaking jump.

Winged Wonders

Flying in formation with just a few skydivers takes skill, practice, and a lot of patience. So getting 71 skydivers to break the largest wingsuit formation record over Lake Elsinore, California, was no walk in the park or, um, fly in the sky. It took five days of solid practice to beat the prestigious Lake Elsinore Wingsuit world record, with the team jumping an incredible 30 times before deciding that they were ready for an official try.

Four airplanes were used in the record attempt, each carrying a team of skydivers who leaped out and then traveled at vertical speeds of 67 mph/109 kmh and forward speeds of 100 mph/161 kmh while managing to fly together in a V formation. There was only 10 feet/3 m separating them before they released their parachutes.

To ensure that they qualified for the record, the German divers had to link arms for three seconds.

Das Country Needz You!

Want to show your patriotism? Display your national pride? Then if you're German, the best way is to throw yourself out of a plane, apparently! In 2008, 200 Germans set a new world record for the most Germans freefalling at the same time and managed to beat the previous record of 156 Germans leaping for their country. And of course, if you really want to impress your fellow citizens, what better way of falling to earth than in the shape and colors of the German flag?

Gone Gaming Crazy

"It was a bit touch-and-go for a while but the gaming community really stepped up to the challenge."
Duncan Best, the London Games Festival's director about beating the previous week-old record by a mere five people.

Zelda, Mario, and Sonic are just a few of the much-loved characters from the brilliant world of video gaming who all got together in 2008. Not in a video game this time, but because British fans dressed up as their favorite video-game characters. There was a reason behind the madness—an attempt to bring together the most fans dressed as video-game characters in one place. The venue was the London Games Festival and 342 fans made the grade, breaking the previous record of 337 set only the week before in Germany!

GAME OVER! The final figure for the nutty gamers assembled for the world record would have been higher but alas, around 50 were given their marching orders because they came dressed up as characters that were more associated with famous films and other media rather than games. Yes, hang your head in shame if you arrived dressed up as Batman—as the rules said, Batman first appeared in a comic book way back in 1939 before debuting in a video game in 1986!

Mad About... Pants?!?

It's not a sight you would usually expect at one of Britain's busiest train stations, but in November 2008, travelers at London's St. Pancras were confronted by 116 people dressed in just their underwear in an attempt to say "Pants To Poverty," the slogan of an organization put together to promote fair-trade products and rights. In the process, the panty-loons made it into the record books for the largest underwear-only gathering ever!

All the crazy-for-pants participants received a free pair of fair-trade pants for their troubles!

Weird Whispers

You'd think that passing a simple message down a line of people might be easy, and that it would go from person to person reliably. But as the game of Chinese Whispers, like the American game of Telephone, shows, what you end up with can be completely different from what you started out with.

This was perfectly illustrated by British children who set a new world record for the longest game of Chinese Whispers. To raise money for charity, 1,330 children were amassed in a London soccer stadium and had to pass the following simple message to one another: "Together we will make a world of difference." This had changed to "Everyone is evil" by the time it had been passed along by 500 children. On reaching the ears of the 1,330th child after two hours, four minutes, the message was simply "Haaaaa." Can we recommend e-mail in the future?

"The person receiving the whisper often becomes anxious and concentrates on the anticipation of receiving the whisper, rather than the whisper itself which results in the misinformation." Joe Jaina, senior lecturer *in organizational behavior, on how the phenomenon of Chinese Whispers works.*

The previous record stood at 1,083 people in 2006, which appropriately enough was set by the Chinese in the city of Chengdu.

Stiletto Sprint!

Men were also spotted during the race sporting rather pretty high heels...

Some women love their stilettos—even, it would seem, when they are running in them. Witness the bizarre sight of 265 Australian women racing against each other in Sydney around a 262-foot/80-m course to break a world record. The winner, Brittney McGlone, was the first to make it to the end of what was a torturous experience for all who ran. After all, the rules were quite clear that all racers must be sporting 3-inch/7.6-cm heels and smooth legs (ask your poor mom about the misery of waxing). Although Brittney must have been delighted with the AUS$5,000 check, she probably wasn't as pleased about winning a pair of highly fashionable high heels. A foot massage followed by a pair of slippers may have been more appropriate...

The previous world record was held by Holland, where only 150 women were crazy enough to run in their fearsome footwear.

"About six girls in front of me fell and two or three heels started spiking up at me," a competitor told Australia's Daily Telegraph newspaper, before revealing an injury.

Utterly Bizarre

Some feats, events, and records defy being placed neatly in a category. So we've rounded up and caged the following out-there bizarre items to form this overwhelmingly weird chapter!

It's hard to imagine why the people in the following pages do what they do. Their ideas and achievements are so wacky that you'll wonder how on earth they dreamed them up in the first place. Whether it's creating a large mechanical spider to march through town (see page 87), discovering you can squirt milk out of your eye (see page 93), or eating your dinner out of a toilet bowl (see page 88), this chapter captures the limitless possibilities of the human imagination. And that's putting it somewhat politely.

So, we recommend that you brace yourself, click your seat belt on, and have a barf bag at the ready (you won't believe what some people eat— see pages 90–91) and prepare to have your mind blown by some of the most crazy, bizarre, and baffling human behavior you'll ever witness. Don't say we didn't warn you...

A Very Peculiar Protester

If you are a protester *and* a performance artist, then you've got to do something a bit more to stand out from an angry crowd. And Mark McGowan knows exactly how to do that.

He's sat in a bath of beans for two weeks in protest at the negativity surrounding the Great British fry-up; he's tried to cartwheel from Brighton to London with two rocks strapped to his feet to protest people taking pebbles from Brighton's beach (and ended up in the hospital); and has eaten a swan in protest of the royal family.

The picture here shows Mark's attempt to "sail" from London to Glasgow in a shopping cart to improve relations between England and Scotland. Sadly, he managed to complete only 65 miles/ 105 km of the 400-mile/644-km journey before he had to give up because of adverse weather conditions. Perhaps he shouldn't have eaten so many of those beans...

Mark once crawled 55 miles/88 km looking for love with a box of chocolates tied to his body and a rose sticking out of his mouth.

"I pushed a monkey nut for seven miles with my nose, from New Cross all the way to 10 Downing Street. I was protesting against student debt."

Mark McGowan on one of his headline-grabbing protest stunts.

The Human Lamp

You would have thought that Zhang Deke from Altay city in China would make the ideal houseguest. After all, he could provide lighting, cooking, and medical treatment without needing to move. The 72-year-old retired highway maintenance man likes to charge himself with 220 volts of electricity as part of his exercise routine, which leaves his body "charged."

He can then place lightbulbs on his head and ears and actually light them (and dim them if you're having a romantic dinner). Zhang is also able to cook a fish on his abdomen in two minutes and has been known to help friends and family with their various ailments such as lumbago, arthritis, and rheumatism with the powers of his electrically charged body.

Zheng has been tested to see how his powers work—in 1994, the Chinese Academy of Sciences examined him and said that he had "a physical dysfunction," but they would not say what it was exactly...

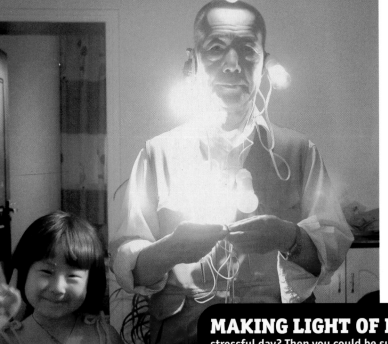

MAKING LIGHT OF IT Do streetlights flicker as you walk past them after a stressful day? Then you could be suffering from Street Light Interference Syndrome. Briton Debbie Wolf claims that the "condition" once caused a line of street lamps to completely fail as she was riding along on a motorbike, drained her TV remote control batteries, and even caused her freezer to defrost. Experts, however, remain unconvinced by the syndrome.

When Spiders Attack!

If you happened to be in Liverpool, England, at the beginning of September 2008, you may well have experienced a heart attack when confronted by a 20-ton spider. Made from wood and steel, the giant arachnid made its way down the streets and over the buildings of the city, voted Capital of Culture 2008. The incredible machine was part of a street theater production that saw the spider, La Princesse, causing a spectacle over a five-day period.

Created by French company La Machine, the $500,000/£250,000 spider is 49 feet/ 15 m high, 65 feet/20 m across, and has 12 people strapped into "her"— they control the spider's 50 axes of movement to create the ultimate in creepy-crawly realism. Bystanders in Liverpool were also soaked by the water that shot out of La Princesse's abdomen. Scary!

The French company responsible for the traffic-stopping spider are no strangers to British streets— their Sultan's Elephant creation saw one million people packing the streets of London as the 50-ton wooden mechanical elephant, operated by 22 people, made its way through Britain's capital.

"I wouldn't like to meet it in the dark." Dorothy Wilson, aged 82, speaks to the U.K. press on how she felt when she first saw the colossal spider.

Most Utterly Bizarre!

Fine dining and luxury hotels are a bit of a cliché, don't you think? Why not try a totally different short break on the wilder side of life...

So, where's the first stop on your weekend of wackiness? Well, Taiwan, of course.

After a long flight, you'll be hungry for some good food, so head straight for the Modern Toilet diner. Its seats are converted toilet bowls, and one of the most popular dishes is ice cream in the shape of dog poop. And before you start thinking that such a restaurant is merely a flash-in-the-toilet-pan idea which will eventually be flushed down the drain, there are already 12 such restaurants in Taipei City, Taiwan.

Ready to rest your weary head? Then hop on a plane over to Germany—next stop is the Alcatraz Hotel, a converted prison in the city of Kaiserslautern. You'll be able to spend the evening in one of its 57 "cells" available to guests to sleep in. You'll spend the night in an original prison bed in traditional prison striped uniforms, sleeping next to the toilet behind a heavy steel door and barred windows. Who knows, you may enjoy it so much you might forget to go home...

If poop doesn't appeal, you could head to the medical-themed DS Music restaurant in Taiwan. There, you'll be served by doctors and nurses while water is served from IV drips mounted in the ceiling.

DOUBLE STAR ENTRY

"People can get striped pajamas, complete with their embroidered name. You can also ask for the prison breakfast, which consists of a small jar of jam, a cup of black coffee, and a piece of pumpernickel bread."

Alcatraz Hotel manager Andreas Kisch.

Bonkers About His 'Bot

To date, Aiko has cost $25,500/ £17,500 to create.

You're looking at the future—an android called Aiko. Scientist Le Trung claims his full-sized robot can recognize faces, give directions, and understand more than 13,000 sentences. Trung spends all his time with her and has been using his life savings to research ways to increase Aiko's abilities. He can often be spotted taking her out for a spin in the countryside and showing off her amazing skills at technology shows.

"I suffered a heart attack and thought that I might need 24-hour care in the future. I may need to have Aiko look after me one day." Le Trung explains why he must perfect his robot creation.

Multitalented Marvel
According to her creator, Aiko has the following features:

- Moves the 24 joints on both her hands
- Remembers a person's name and face
- Learns directions and judges what the weather is like
- Distinguishes different types of food and drink

Performing Pests

Many people think that they are fantasy, but flea circuses, where tiny insects perform amazing feats, are real, and you can still go to see one. The Floh-Circus held every October at the beer festival in Munich, Germany, is home to a show where fleas are put through their paces across a wide range of disciplines. These include flea soccer, where the insect "kicks" a tiny ball into a net and, pictured here, the feat of flea-powered chariot races, where three fleas try to, well, out-flee each other and win. The dog fleas used weigh just 0.2 milligrams and are able to pull objects that are an astonishing 20,000 times heavier than themselves.

TOUGH JOB The life of a flea athlete is not an easy one—the fleas live for about a year, six months of which is taken up by the flea reaching the right maturity before embarking on three months of training and then three months of actual performing to the paying public. Their reward? A constant supply of fresh blood to feed on, direct from the hands of their trainers. Mmm, tasty.

Funny Foods of the World

We like our food "normal" in the West and preferably with a side order of fries. But to people from other continents, our tastes must seem very bland...

Take the Japanese, who enjoy the dangerous delicacy Fugu globefish (pictured right). A deadly toxin can be found throughout the fish's body—in its organs, membrane, and even its skin. To be able to eat the fish and actually survive requires the skills of a specially licensed chef. It costs up to 20,000 yen (about $218.00 or £150) to enjoy the thrill.

FRIED CAMBODIAN SPIDERS

SPIDER MAN To cook the perfect spider, panfry it with salt and garlic. When its skin has turned deep red-brown, eat it hot—ideally, the fried spider should be crisp on the outside but juicy on the inside. Bon appetit!

A rather outlandish Southeast Asian treat is the Cambodian spider (pictured left), which is a huge seller in its homeland because it is now regarded as a delicacy. The nation first turned to the spider for nutrition in the 1970s when refugees forced themselves to eat them to stay alive. The spiders, which breed in holes in the ground, look similar to tarantulas and are fried in woks at local markets. Although poisonous when alive, the spider's venom is rendered harmless once cooked, and eating the eight-legged critter is supposed to have medicinal benefits too—Cambodians say that it can help with coughs, backache, and breathing problems. Cambodia's other national delicacy, the garlic-fried cricket, may leave some tourists running for the hills at mealtime...

CRISPY GARLIC CRICKETS

As well as spiders, Cambodians also enjoy a more lively critter—crickets. Should you find yourself in Cambodia in the month of June, expect to see farmers out in full force with nets and high-powered ultra-violet lights in their fields during the "cricket season," where they catch newly hatched insects. These are bought by market vendors who fry the insects with garlic for hungry customers (pictured right).

Finally, if you should find yourself further south, driving down the roads of Malawi, Africa, why not pull over and enjoy the local delicacy of a mouse-on-a-stick? For a 100 Malawian Kwacha (53.5¢ US), you can buy a dried-out mouse (pictured left) as a tasty example of African fast food. Hungry readers will be pleased to note that the head, skin, bones, and intestines are all included in the price! You lucky people.

MOUSE MANNERS

The proper way to eat a mouse on a stick is by beginning with the tail and working your way up to the head, spitting out the bones as you go. A bit like a furry, crunchy chicken wing.

Freak School

Forget studying history or plowing through the works of Shakespeare—for those of you wanting a truly unique education, you may want to enroll at the Coney Island Sideshow School in Brooklyn, New York, and be taught how to be a circus performer in seven days. That means learning the art of sword swallowing, glass walking, lying on a bed of nails, breathing fire, escaping from a straitjacket while hanging upside down and, as pictured here, how to hammer a spike into your head without dying instantly.

The teacher who runs the weeklong course is the charmingly named Donny Vomit, who's been tossing chain saws and electrocuting people in his freaky electric chair for more than a decade.

"Be a freak in just one week!" the Coney Island Sideshow School motto.

According to self-confessed freak Donny Vomit, there are three kinds of freak:

Natural Freaks
• Natural performers who are born the way they are, such as bearded ladies.

Man-Made Freaks
• Self-made freaks such as those with huge numbers of tattoos or who have weird and wonderful piercings over their bodies.

Working Freaks
• Those freaks who have learned to be freaks by acquiring a "skill" such as bashing a nail into one's head. This is known as a performance more than anything else. Just sounds plain painful to us.

Hissing and Kissing

Snake charmer Khum Chaibuddee must be crazy; it's the only explanation for his decision to attempt to break the world record for the most venomous snakes ever kissed, in October 2006. His Thai audience must have held their collective breaths as king cobras were individually released and then slithered their way on to the special staging area to be confronted by Khum with his puckered-up lips at the ready. Nineteen snakes later and Khum had finished, warning the children in the audience not to attempt the same feat at home. Wise words.

The previous record of 11 snakes kissed was set by Gordon Cates from the U.S. back in 1999.

For Khum's safety, medics were on standby to administer a serum if one of the cobras decided it didn't want to be kissed.

HOW DANGEROUS? Its venom may not be the most potent—that honor goes to the sea snake—but the king cobra can inject so much venom when it gets its fangs into you that it can kill an elephant, never mind a snake-charming human being.

Milk Man

Turkish construction worker Ilker Yilmaz found out he had a special gift while he was swimming. No, it wasn't the ability to breathe underwater or to detect pee in the pool; he noticed that he squirted water out of his eye. The logical thing to do next then was to see just what else he could squirt out of his eye and over what distance.

So in 2004 at the Armada Hotel in Istanbul, Ilker wowed (and grossed out) audiences by snorting milk up his nose and then, on his third attempt, shooting out a 9.1-foot/2.8-m squirt of milk from his left eye. He beat the previous world record holder, Mike Moraal of Canada, who had set the world record for milk squirting with an impressive 8.5 feet/2.6 m in 2001.

The amazing Ilker managed to put out five lit candles in under two minutes using his amazing milk-shooting ability.

"I'm happy and proud that I can get Turkey in the record book even if it's for milk squirting," world record holder Ilker Yilmaz explains.

Scorpion Queen

Five thousand scorpions. Thirty-three days. A 10-square-foot/3-sq-m glass box. Thai Kanchana Ketkaew deserves her title of Scorpion Queen after she set a world record in January 2009 for spending the most time confined with poisonous scorpions. And she's no stranger to them either—her previous record was set in 2002, when she lived with 3,400 of the pincer-wielding horrors for 32 days.

The Scorpion Queen endured being stung by the scorpions 13 times during her record-breaking attempt. After five years of exposing herself to scorpion stings during training, her body is able to fight the ill effects of the scorpion poison, but visitors reported seeing Kanchana tearful at times. Well, spending so much time in a glass box being watched by both the scorpions and the public can't have been easy. Madness, then, that she has vowed to return to her glass room again if someone tries to challenge her record.

"It's very difficult but I tried because I received a lot of support from Thais and foreign tourists in the past 33 days," Scorpion Queen Kanchana Ketkaew said, on breaking her 2002 world record.

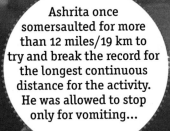

Ashrita once somersaulted for more than 12 miles/19 km to try and break the record for the longest continuous distance for the activity. He was allowed to stop only for vomiting...

Meet Mr. Record Breaker

Most people would be happy to break one record in their lifetime. Unless, of course, it's beaten the following year. And if it was, then there's every chance that it would be beaten by Ashrita Furman, who is the world record holder for...well...holding the most records.

He has set 183 world records and currently holds 76 records across a staggering range of disciplines. His records include snapping 94 bananas in a minute; crushing 53 eggs on his head in 30 seconds; juggling underwater for 48 minutes and 36 seconds; and pushing a car the farthest in 24 hours (17 miles/27.4 km). Ashrita has broken records in 30 countries over the past 25 years. It's a mystery how he finds time to serve customers at the New York health food store he manages.

"If the stunt won't give you some joy, forget about it. A big part of setting a world record is to have a lot of fun!" Ashrita Furman offers advice to wannabe record breakers in the book Tricks of the Trade for Kids.

In the picture shown here, Ashrita attempted to beat his own record for the longest time spent juggling underwater with three balls. He boasted the previous record of 48 minutes and 36 seconds, which he set in New Zealand in 2002. Alas, for his second record attempt in Malaysia, Ashrita made it to 37 minutes and 45 seconds before the large shark in the background bumped into him, causing him to drop one of the balls. Not a bad excuse, really.

RECORD OF ACHIEVEMENT
Here are some of Ashrita's other records. Want to try beating any of them yourself?

Milk Bottle Balancing on Head—longest continuous distance—80.7 miles/130.27 km (set in April 1998, USA)

Duct Taping Oneself to a Wall—fastest time— 8 minutes and 7 seconds (set in January 2008, USA)

Balancing Eggs on Their Ends—most simultaneously balancing—700 (set in November 2006, USA)

Norman has wrangled bees for movies such as the Oscar-nominated *Fried Green Tomatoes*, the first X-Files movie, and *Invasion of the Bee Girls* in 1973.

Bee-Movie Star

That clarinet isn't just for show—Norman has played professionally for more than 45 years.

Playing the clarinet while covered in bees is just one of Norman Gary's amazing tricks. He has also appeared on more than 70 television shows, done six commercials featuring bees, and been a bee wrangler for 18 films—meaning he trains and takes care of bees when they are required to perform in front of the cameras. On top of all that, he also set a world record when he held 109 bees in his closed mouth for 10 seconds while they feasted on a sugar-syrup-soaked sponge!

"People ask me from time to time if I get stung by the bees that I work with, and the answer is 'yes.' Whenever I make a mistake I get stung, so the stings can be prevented if you're very careful," explains Norman Gary.

Tiana's slippery snail days are now behind her—what she really wants to do is become an Olympic gymnast. Here's hoping she can move faster than her slimy chums!

Snail Bait!

One minute you're just a nine-year-old schoolgirl called Tiana Walton, the next you're a world record holder for having the most snails sliming their way all over your face—25 of them in fact! The rules for setting the record were strict but simple: Tiana had to put that many snails on her face as she could in one minute, then had to tip her head forward—any snails that fell off over a ten-second period were disallowed. Her 25 snail count beat the previous record of 15, and her mom, Tommy, must be proud—after all, she set the world record in 1980 for growing the world's largest lemon!

"I am not squeamish. It is relaxing but it feels a bit cold. They are quite smelly and you can see their big long eyes," Tiana Walton explains.

After their epic ordeal, the snails were treated to a gourmet meal.